Juanderful Life: The Titanic Series

Seeing Beyond the Shipwreck to a New Horizon

Juanderful Life: The Titanic Series – Seeing Beyond the Shipwreck to a New Horizon

Published by Jackie Boatwright Publishing
An imprint of Juanderful Holdings LLC, Atlanta, Georgia, USA

This book is a work of inspiration and leadership development. The names, events, and reflections are drawn from the author's personal experiences, professional insights, and spiritual revelation. Any resemblance to actual persons, living or deceased, is coincidental and unintentional.

Printed in the United States of America ISBN:
978-0-9725295-5-6

Library of Congress Control Number Applied for

Cover Design: Jackie Boatwright Publishing.

Publisher: Jackie Boatwright Publishing.
For information, inquiries, or speaking engagements:
jackie@juanderfulenterprises.com
www.jackieboatwright.com

Scriptures, quotes, and references are used under fair use for educational and inspirational purposes. All scripture quotations, unless otherwise indicated, are taken from the Holy Bible, King James Version.

Dedication

To Amarie and Ivy,

My heart's joy, and two beautiful reminders that the future is always worth building for.

I dedicate this book to you with the hope that as you grow, you will become resilient, faithful, wise, brave, and deeply rooted in who God created you to be.

May you learn early that life will not always be easy, but you are never without strength. May you understand that storms may come, plans may change, and seasons may shift, but none of those things have the power to define your whole story.

May you grow into women who know how to stand with grace, think with clarity, love with courage, and keep your eyes lifted toward the horizon God has placed before you.

And may you always remember that when life tilts, you can breathe, pray, rise, and keep moving forward.

With all my love,

Momma

THE UNSHAKABLE LEADER

by Jacqueline Boatwright-Daus, BS, MBA, Ed.S.,
Founder of Juanderful Leadership

The Journey Toward a Juanderful Life

This is not a book about living untouched. It is a book about living awake. Life has a way of shifting without asking permission. One moment, things appear steady. The next moment, something changes. A call comes. A door closes. A relationship strains. A plan breaks. A season ends before you were ready to release it. And suddenly, you are standing in a life that still looks familiar on the outside, while something inside you is trying to find ground.

That is where this journey begins. Not at the end of the storm. Not after every question has been answered. Not when your emotions are perfectly settled and your next steps are completely clear. It begins in the honest place where you admit, "Something has shifted, and I need to learn how to move from here."

A Juanderful Life is not a perfect life. It is a well navigated life. It is a life rooted in faith, guided by purpose, strengthened by discipline, softened by peace, and lived with enough presence to recognize when your soul needs attention. It is not measured by how little you have endured. It is measured by how faithfully you learn to live through what you have endured. This book is organized as a journey.

In **The Tilt**, you will recognize the moments when life shifts, when fear narrows your vision, when drift begins quietly, and when "I'm fine" becomes a place to hide.

In **Navigation**, you will learn how to make decisions when emotions are unreliable, how to prioritize what matters, how to move before conditions are perfect, and how to remain steady when others depend on you.

In **The Return**, you will come back to yourself, to peace, to faith, and to the inner places that pressure may have covered but could not destroy.

In **The Horizon**, you will learn to live forward with alignment, focus, presence, gratitude, and vision.

You do not have to read this book from a place of perfection.

Bring your questions.

Bring your weariness.

Bring your faith, even if it feels small.

Bring the parts of your life that still feel unfinished.

The goal is not to pretend the storm never happened.

The goal is to become more awake, more grounded, more faithful, and more intentional because of what you have learned. Your story is not over. The tilt is not the end.

There is still a horizon ahead. And step by step, breath by breath, decision by decision, you can begin moving toward a life that is not merely survived but truly lived.

A Juanderful Life.

PART I: THE TILT

Chapter 1

OPENING HORIZON

A Moment When Life Tilts

This book is for the person standing in a life that still looks normal on the outside, while everything inside them is trying to find ground.

On a Tuesday that began like any other, the phone rang. The coffee was still warm. The calendar was open on the kitchen table. Morning light stretched across the floor in that quiet way light does when the day has not yet been interrupted. There were ordinary things around me. A pen. A mug. A list. A few small plans for later. Nothing looked different. That is what makes some moments so unsettling.

Life does not always announce change with noise. Sometimes it enters through something ordinary. A phone call. A sentence. A pause before someone says what they really mean. The voice on the other end was careful. Too careful.

There are tones people use when they are trying to place hard news gently into your hands. I heard that tone before I understood the words.

Restructure.

Uncertainty.

We will need to talk soon.

I stood still. Not because I was calm. Because my mind had moved faster than my body. In a matter of seconds, the future began rearranging itself. Bills. Responsibilities. People depending on me. Plans I had trusted. Doors I thought were open. The quiet question that rises before you are ready to answer it:

What now? The coffee was still there. The calendar was still there. The morning was still moving as if nothing had happened. But inside me, something had shifted. That is how the tilt often begins. Not with a dramatic collapse. Not always with an audience. Not always with words large enough for other people to understand.

Sometimes the tilt is private. You are standing in the same room, holding the same phone, wearing the same expression, but inwardly, you know the ground beneath your life no longer feels the same.

For a moment, I did not need a strategy. I needed breath. I needed to stay present long enough not to let fear write the ending before the story had unfolded. Because fear is quick.

It does not wait for facts. It does not ask for wisdom. It rushes ahead, gathers every possible loss, and brings them back to you as if they are already true. That morning, fear tried to do what fear often does. It tried to shrink the future. It tried to turn one uncertain conversation into a complete conclusion. It tried to make me believe that because something had shifted, everything was lost.

But something quieter was also present. Not loud, not dramatic, nor fully formed. Just a small inner knowing that this moment was real, but it was not the whole story.

That is where a Juanderful Life begins. Not when everything is easy, not when every answer is clear, nor when the horizon is visible. It begins in the moment when life tilts and you choose not to surrender your whole future to the first wave of fear.

Fear can warn you. Panic can drown you. When life tilts, panic demands immediate certainty. It wants guarantees, explanations, and instant solutions.

The paradox is this: The moment you accept that the storm is real, you finally gain footing. Not because the situation improves instantly, but because acceptance allows you to stop wasting energy pretending the waters are calm. Denial delays response. Acceptance creates movement.

This is where many people become trapped. They wait to feel motivated before taking action. They wait to feel confident before making decisions. They wait to feel emotionally settled before rebuilding. But seasoned navigators understand something others do not: Direction matters more than emotion.

This is why seeing beyond the horizon is not optimism. It is discipline. It is the practice of refusing to let present instability blind you to future possibilities.

The horizon itself is an interesting thing. You never fully arrive at it. As you move forward, it moves forward too. Yet sailors still depend on it for direction. In the same way, vision is not about reaching a perfect destination where difficulty disappears forever. Vision is about maintaining direction while conditions change around you.

Many people lose years of their lives waiting for fear to disappear. Wise leaders learn to move while fear is still sitting in the room. That lesson changes everything. It changes how you respond to financial pressure.

How you handle disappointment.
How you recover from betrayal.

How you lead your family.
How you rebuild after failure.
How you make decisions when the future feels unclear.

You do not need to become fearless to survive a storm. You need to become steady. Steadiness is built through repeated decisions. Small acts of discipline repeated long enough to create internal stability. This is not glamorous work. It will not always look impressive from the outside.

The question is never whether storms will come. The question is whether you will know how to navigate when they do.

A Juanderful Life is not a perfect life. It is a life lived with vision, discipline, faith, resilience, and purpose. It is a life that learns how to remain emotionally anchored, spiritually grounded, and intentionally directed when circumstances tilt unexpectedly.

It is not about avoiding pain. It is about learning how to move through it with courage, clarity, and a steady hand.

Chapter 2

THE HORIZON SHIFT

What Happens Internally When Life Shifts

There is a quiet confusion that comes when life changes faster than your heart can process. Your body understands something has shifted before your mind has language for it. The chest tightens. The breath becomes shallow. Thoughts begin moving too quickly, each one reaching for certainty and finding none. You may stand completely still on the outside while internally everything is searching for something solid to hold.

This is the strange beginning of disruption. Not always panic. Sometimes it is silence. Sometimes it is the sudden inability to finish an ordinary task.

You look at the same room, the same calendar, the same cup on the table, but everything feels slightly unfamiliar. The objects have not changed. The walls have not moved. The morning has not announced itself differently.

But something inside you knows the meaning of the moment has changed. That is what instability does first. It interrupts your inner rhythm.

It takes the life you thought you were walking through and makes you question the ground beneath it. Plans that felt reliable become uncertain. Conversations you expected to have later suddenly feel urgent. Small responsibilities begin carrying larger emotional weight. The mind begins reaching forward.

What happens now?

What does this mean?

How long will this last?

What if this becomes worse?

Fear rarely waits for facts before it begins building possibilities. It moves quickly. It fills empty spaces with imagined outcomes. It turns unanswered questions into heavy conclusions. It convinces the body to prepare for danger, even when all you have received is information.

And this is where many people begin to lose themselves. Not because the situation has fully unfolded. But because the internal reaction becomes louder than the reality in front of them.

A life shift does not only change circumstances. It changes atmosphere. The same home can feel different after one phone call. The same job can feel uncertain after one meeting. The same relationship can feel fragile after one conversation.

The same future can feel distant after one unexpected turn. And when atmosphere changes, people often begin making emotional agreements with fear before they realize it.

They agree to worry.

They agree to brace.

They agree to assume the worst.

They agree to carry tomorrow before tomorrow arrives.

This is why the first moments after disruption matter so deeply. Not because you must have an answer immediately. But because you must notice what is happening inside you before fear begins quietly leading you.

A Juanderful Life is not built by pretending those moments do not shake you. It is built by learning how to remain present when they do.

Presence does not mean you feel calm instantly. It means you stop long enough to recognize: Something has shifted. I am afraid. I do not have all the answers yet. But I do not have to surrender my entire inner life to this moment.

That recognition is powerful. It creates a small space between what happened and who you become in response. And sometimes that small space is where wisdom begins.

The Horizon Shift: Training Your Eyes Beyond the Storm

A discouraged person can walk into a room full of opportunity and notice only risk. An exhausted person can interpret temporary delays as permanent failure. Someone carrying disappointment for too long can slowly lose the ability to imagine a future different from their present circumstances.

Pressure alters perception. And perception influences decision-making long before circumstances actually improve or decline. That is why two people can experience the same disruption and emerge completely different. One becomes consumed by reaction. The other becomes more intentional. One loses clarity. The other develops discernment. The difference is rarely intelligence. It is perspective.

The greatest danger during instability is not always the disruption itself. Sometimes it's losing the ability to see beyond it.

Most people believe difficult seasons primarily test strength. In reality, they often test vision. They test whether you can maintain direction while your emotions are trying to convince you that everything is collapsing.

Fear has a way of shrinking the future. When fear enters the room, the future often becomes smaller. Not because the future has actually disappeared, but because fear reduces what the mind is able to imagine. Possibility narrows. Hope feels less believable. Options that once seemed available begin to feel unrealistic or far away.

A person who once dreamed with confidence may suddenly begin thinking only in terms of survival. The question changes from "What am I building?" to "How do I get through this?" And while survival may be necessary for a season, it was never meant to become the entire vision for a life.

Fear has a way of convincing people that the present moment is permanent. It whispers that this difficulty will always feel this heavy. That this uncertainty will always be this loud. That this disappointment has already decided the ending. But fear is not a prophet. It does not know the whole story. It only knows how to interpret pain loudly.

This is why people must be careful about making permanent decisions from temporary fear. A frightened mind may want to quit too soon, close too tightly, speak too harshly, or retreat too completely.

Not because the person lacks wisdom, but because fear has shortened the distance between discomfort and decision.

A Juanderful Life needs a wider view. It asks you to pause long enough to remember that what you feel today is real, but it may not be final.

That one closed door does not mean every door is closed. That one hard season does not mean your life has lost direction. That one disappointment does not have permission to define the entire horizon.

When fear shrinks the future, faith helps widen it again. Not by pretending the problem is small. But by reminding you that the problem is not all there is.

Faith gives the soul room to breathe when circumstances feel tight. It reminds you that you are not required to solve the whole future in one frightened moment. Sometimes you only need enough steadiness for the next honest step.

That step may be small.

A phone call.

A prayer.

A pause.

A conversation.

A decision not to spiral.

A decision not to quit.

A decision to wait until peace returns before choosing from panic.

This is why emotionally overwhelmed people often make decisions that deepen instability instead of resolving it. They react prematurely. They abandon meaningful goals too quickly. They confuse temporary discomfort with permanent failure.

Pressure distorts proportion. A setback starts feeling like a dead end. A closed door feels like rejection. A slow season feels like proof that nothing is working. But perception under pressure is not always trustworthy.

Emotionally mature people understand this. They allow themselves to feel disappointment without allowing disappointment to become their identity. They recognize fear without placing fear in charge of decision-making. They understand uncertainty without assuming uncertainty means hopelessness. That balance is difficult. Especially when life feels tilted and when answers are incomplete.

But this is where the horizon shift begins. Not when circumstances suddenly improve. Not when clarity fully returns. The shift begins the moment you decide that your present condition will not become the boundary of your vision. That decision changes how people move through adversity.

Instead of asking:
Why is this happening?

They begin asking:
How do I move wisely from here?

Instead of becoming emotionally consumed by what is unstable, they begin strengthening what can still be built. Their thinking becomes steadier. Less reactive. More intentional. Because seeing beyond the storm is not denial. It is disciplined perspective. It is the refusal to make permanent conclusions from temporary emotions.

This matters because people rarely destroy their lives in one dramatic moment. More often, decline happens slowly through repeated emotionally driven decisions. Fear shortens vision.

Discouragement weakens discipline. Frustration creates impulsive thinking. Eventually, people stop responding strategically and start living entirely from emotional survival. But survival alone is not the goal.

A Juanderful Life is not built merely by enduring hardship. It is built by learning how to navigate hardship without losing direction. That requires training your eyes differently.

It requires learning how to separate current discomfort from future possibilities. It requires understanding that not every delay is failure and not every difficult season is destruction.

Some seasons are revealing what needs strengthening. Some are correcting misalignment. Some are teaching patience, discernment, and discipline in ways comfort never could.

Growth rarely feels glamorous while it is happening. Most transformation happens quietly. The willingness to continue moving responsibly even when certainty has not fully arrived. This is why perspective matters so deeply.

Perspective determines whether pressure refines you or consumes you. Two people can experience the same disruption and walk away with entirely different futures. One becomes bitter, reactive, and emotionally exhausted. The other becomes wiser, steadier, and more intentional.

Again, the difference is rarely intelligence. It is perspective. And perspective is trainable. You can train yourself to pause before reacting. To evaluate before assuming. To think beyond the moment instead of becoming imprisoned by it. To remain grounded while emotions rise. To continue building even when visibility is limited. That is the horizon shift.

The moment you stop allowing fear to define what you are capable of seeing. The moment you realize that uncertainty may surround you without needing to control you. The moment you understand that direction still exists even when the path ahead is not fully visible.

Because the people who moved forward in life are rarely the people who avoided every storm. They are the people who learned how to see beyond them.

The Difference Between Hope and Vision

Hope and vision are related, but they are not the same. Hope says, "I believe better is possible." Vision says, "I am willing to move in the direction of better, even before I can see the whole path."

Hope comforts the heart. Vision organizes life. Hope gives you something to hold. Vision gives you somewhere to go.

There are seasons when hope is enough to keep a person from giving up. That matters. Sometimes the soul needs a small light, a quiet reminder, a reason to believe the present moment is not the final chapter. But hope without vision can become passive. It can wait endlessly for life to change while making no internal shift, no practical adjustment, no courageous decision.

Vision requires participation. It asks something of you. It asks you to become attentive to your choices. To notice what you keep repeating. To ask whether your daily life is carrying you toward the future you say you desire. A Juanderful Life needs both.

Hope keeps the spirit tender. Vision keeps life directed. Without hope, vision can become harsh and mechanical. Without vision, hope can become sentimental and inactive. Together, they create movement with meaning.

This is why seeing beyond the storm is not simply about believing things will get better. It is about living today in a way that makes better possible.

Sometimes that begins quietly. You stop rehearsing the worst outcome. You return to one responsibility you can handle. You choose one honest conversation. You protect one hour of peace. You take one step that agrees with the future, instead of the fear. That is vision.

A person with vision does not need perfect conditions to begin. They understand that clarity often grows after movement, not before it. And sometimes, the future becomes visible only after you take the next faithful step.

Permanent Decisions from Temporary Emotions

Temporary emotions can feel permanent while you are inside them. Anger can make one conversation feel like the whole relationship.

Fear can make one setback feel like the end of the road. Exhaustion can make every responsibility feel impossible. Disappointment can make the future feel already decided. This is why some of the most important decisions in life require a pause. A sacred space between feeling and choosing.

Many people have made decisions from pain that they later had to heal from. They left too quickly. Spoke too sharply. Quit too soon. Closed their hearts too tightly. Assumed an ending when life was only asking for adjustment. The emotion was real. But it was not the whole truth.

A Juanderful Life calls for learning the difference between what you feel deeply and what you should decide permanently.

Feelings deserve attention. They carry information. They tell you when something hurts, when something matters, when something feels unsafe, when something needs care. But feelings are not always wise enough to be given final authority. Especially when they are fresh and when they are loud. Especially if the feelings are born from fear, exhaustion, humiliation, grief, or disappointment.

There is a kind of wisdom that does not rush to decide while the soul is still shaking. It waits for the waters inside to settle enough to see clearly. Sometimes the most powerful thing you can say is:

I need time before I decide.

I need quiet before I respond.

I need peace before I make this permanent.

That pause can protect your future.

It can protect relationships.

It can protect your purpose.

It can protect you from confusing a hard moment with a final conclusion. Not every emotional urge deserves immediate obedience. Some feelings need to be heard. Some need to be held.

Some feelings need to be prayed through. Some need to pass before they are interpreted. A well-navigated life is not a life without emotion. It is a life where emotion is honored without being allowed to steer everything.

That is not coldness. That is maturity. And maturity often looks like waiting until your whole self is present before making a decision your future self will have to live with.

Chapter 3

RECOGNIZING THE DRIFT

The Drift Before the Damage

There are seasons in life when nothing appears broken from the outside, yet something inside you knows you are no longer fully aligned.

You still show up. Still answer emails. Still smile in conversations. Still complete responsibilities. But beneath the routine, there is a quiet disconnection that is difficult to explain.

Sometimes it begins as exhaustion, as restlessness, as the strange feeling of moving constantly, while no longer feeling connected to where you are going.

The unsettling part about drift is that it rarely announces itself dramatically. Most people do not wake up one morning completely lost. More often, they slowly stop listening to themselves in small and almost unnoticeable ways.

They postpone rest. Ignore tension. Silence conviction. Adapt to stress, they were never meant to normalize.

Little by little, survival replaces presence. And eventually, they look up and realize they have spent years managing life without deeply living it.

That realization can be painful. Not because life has completely fallen apart, but because some part of you remembers that you were created for more than emotional survival.

A Juanderful Life is not built by pretending everything is beautiful all the time. It is built by remaining connected to what is true even while life feels demanding, uncertain, or heavy.

Sometimes the greatest threat to a meaningful life is not catastrophe. Sometimes it is unconscious living. The slow habit of disconnecting from your own spirit while remaining productive enough to avoid confronting it. Sometimes the first sign of healing is not a dramatic change. Sometimes it is simply noticing yourself again.

Noticing what drains you.

What restores you.

What no longer feels honest.

What you have been tolerating for too long.

What your spirit keeps trying to say beneath all the noise.

Many people spend years overriding themselves. They override exhaustion. Override grief. Override intuition and override peace. Until eventually they no longer know the difference between who they are and who they became to survive. A Juanderful Life asks you to return. Not to an older version of yourself. But to a truer one.

What Drift Feels Like in Daily Life

Drift does not always feel like crisis. Sometimes it feels like waking up already tired. Like moving through the day with a body that is present but a spirit that feels somewhere else.

Like answering messages, you do not have the emotional space to answer. Like sitting in a room with people you love and still feeling strangely distant.

Drift can feel like losing interest in things that once restored you. Music does not reach you the same way. Prayer feels harder to settle into. Laughter comes, but not as freely.

Rest is available, but you do not know how to receive it. You keep doing what needs to be done, but something inside you feels less alive while doing it.

That is what makes drift difficult to name. Nothing may be visibly wrong. You may still be responsible. Still productive. Still kind. Still capable. Still showing up.

But inwardly, you sense a quiet separation between the life you are living and the life you are meant to inhabit.

Sometimes drift sounds like:

I will deal with that later.

I do not have time to feel this.

I just need to get through the week.

I cannot stop right now.

I am fine.

Those sentences may seem harmless at first. Sometimes they are necessary. But repeated long enough, they can become a way of disappearing from yourself. A Juanderful Life necessitates noticing when you are no longer fully present in your own life.

Noticing when you have become more committed to functioning than feeling. More committed to managing than meaning. More committed to keeping peace around you than cultivating peace within you.

This kind of noticing is tender work. It does not require self-condemnation. It requires honesty. Because drift is not proof that you have failed. Sometimes drift is simply evidence that some part of you has been waiting too long to be heard.

The Difference Between Being Productive and Being Present

Productivity can make a person look alive, while presence reveals whether they are truly connected to living. There is nothing wrong with being productive. Responsibilities matter. Work matters. Commitments matter.

There are seasons when discipline is necessary, when things must be handled, when people depend on your consistency. But productivity becomes dangerous when it replaces presence.

You can complete tasks and still feel absent from your own life. You can answer every message and still ignore the quiet message rising inside you.

You can manage a household, run a business, serve a community, care for others, and still not know when you last felt deeply at home within yourself. Presence is different. Presence asks you to notice. To feel. To breathe. To listen inwardly before the world tells you what it needs next.

Presence is the ability to inhabit the life you are living instead of merely maintaining it. A productive life may look impressive from the outside. A present life feels honest from the inside. That distinction matters. Because a Juanderful Life is not measured only by how much you accomplish.

It is measured by whether you remain connected to purpose, faith, joy, and truth while you are accomplishing it. Some people are praised for their output while privately grieving their disconnection. They are admired for capacity but starving for stillness.

They are applauded for strength but longing for softness. They keep producing because production gives them evidence that they are still useful. But usefulness is not the same as wholeness. And being needed is not the same as being nourished.

There comes a time when the soul begins asking for more than completion. It asks for connection. Not just with others. With yourself. With God. With the quiet truth beneath the noise. That is why presence is not laziness. Presence is alignment.

It is the sacred practice of returning to the life you are actually living and asking whether your pace, choices, and commitments still agree with the person you are becoming.

A Juanderful Life needs that kind of return. Again, and again. Not because productivity is wrong. But because productivity without presence can become a polished form of disappearance.

The Cost of Unconscious Living

Unconscious living rarely feels dangerous while it is happening. It often feels practical. Necessary. Normal.

You wake up, move through responsibilities, respond to what is urgent, and repeat the same patterns because repetition can create the illusion of stability. Days become routines. Routines become identity. Identity becomes something you stop questioning because questioning it would require stillness. And stillness can be frightening when you have spent years outrunning your own truth.

Unconscious living is not always reckless. Sometimes it is highly organized. The calendar is full. The bills are paid. The obligations are met. The image is maintained.

But somewhere beneath the appearance of order, a quieter life remains unattended. The cost is subtle at first.

You stop noticing what brings you joy.

You stop questioning what drains you.

You stop listening when your spirit feels unsettled.

You stop asking whether the life you are maintaining is still the life you are meant to inhabit.

Over time, unconscious living creates distance. Distance from peace. Distance from purpose. Distance from God. Distance from your own inner voice.

You may still be moving, but movement without awareness can become a form of wandering. A Juanderful Life cannot be lived unconsciously. It asks for attention. It asks you to notice when you are saying yes out of habit instead of conviction.

When you are staying busy to avoid grief.

When you are accepting pressure as normal simply because you have carried it for so long.

When you are mistaking survival for obedience.

When you are building a life that looks impressive but feels unfamiliar to your spirit.

That kind of noticing can be uncomfortable, but discomfort is not always an enemy. Sometimes discomfort is the part of you that still remembers the truth.

It is the inner signal that says: This pace is costing me something. This pattern no longer feels right internally. This version of me was necessary for survival, but it cannot become my permanent home.

The danger of unconscious living is not only that you may lose time. It is that you may slowly lose tenderness, wonder, discernment, and joy. The ability to hear yourself clearly. The ability to recognize when God is calling you toward something deeper than routine.

A life can become efficient and still lose its sense of sacredness. That is a high cost. Because a Juanderful Life is not simply a life that works. It is a life that is awake to truth, to purpose, and to peace.

Awake to the quiet places inside you that still need care. And sometimes awakening begins with one honest admission: I have been living on autopilot, and I am ready to come back to myself.

What People Silently Carry

Not all weight is visible. Some of the heaviest things people carry cannot be seen from the outside at all. Unspoken disappointment. Private grief. Resentment that never found language. Pressure that has lasted too long. The exhaustion of constantly being strong for everyone else.

Many people learn how to function while emotionally overloaded. They go to work. Attend meetings and answer messages. They care for families, smile in conversations, and handle responsibilities. From the outside, they appear capable and composed. But internally, they are carrying more than they were ever meant to carry alone.

This is one of the strange realities of adulthood. As people grow older, they often become increasingly skilled at hiding themselves. Not intentionally at first. It simply becomes easier to say "I'm fine" than to explain the complexity of what is actually happening inside.

So, people continue moving through life while quietly carrying things that are slowly becoming heavier. Old disappointments, unresolved hurt; Words they never healed from or dreams they abandoned but never grieved.

They carry versions of themselves they had to become to survive difficult seasons. Over time, emotional weight changes people. Not always dramatically, but subtly. It shortens patience. Weakens joy, creates irritability, makes rest feel difficult; Makes trust feel dangerous and softness feel unsafe.

Some people become emotionally distant not because they lack love, but because carrying too much for too long has made openness feel exhausting. Others become overly productive because staying busy temporarily distracts them from what they have not processed internally.

Pain does not always look emotional. Sometimes it looks efficient. Sometimes it looks independent. Sometimes it looks like the person everyone admires for "holding everything together."

But constantly holding everything together can quietly break something inside a person if they never allow themselves space to breathe, grieve, rest, or tell the truth about what they are carrying.

A Juanderful Life calls for honesty about emotional weight. Not dramatic honesty. Not performative vulnerability. Just truth. The kind of truth that says:

This hurt me more than I admitted.
I have been stronger than people realize.
I am tired in places that rest alone cannot fix.
Something inside me needs care, not avoidance.

That kind of honesty can feel uncomfortable, especially for people who have spent most of their lives surviving. Survival teaches people to suppress. To compartmentalize. To move forward quickly because stopping might feel unsafe.

But ignored emotional weight does not disappear. It settles. And whatever settles internally eventually shapes how a person sees the world.

A person carrying unresolved disappointment may begin expecting rejection before it arrives.

A person carrying betrayal may struggle to trust even healthy relationships.

A person carrying years of emotional exhaustion may stop believing joy is sustainable.

This is why some people become hardened without fully noticing it happening. Not because they are cruel. Because they are tired. There is a difference.

A hardened heart is often a tired heart that stayed unprotected for too long. That realization should create compassion, not shame.

Because many people are carrying burdens they never fully chose. Family pressure. Financial strain. Caregiving. Loss. Loneliness. Expectations. Silent heartbreak. The emotional cost of constantly showing up for others while privately feeling unseen themselves.

Some people have not had a deep breath emotionally in years. And yet they continue functioning because life keeps requiring things from them. This is where many people begin confusing survival with living. But a Juanderful Life is more than survival.

It is not merely the ability to endure pressure while becoming emotionally numb in the process. It is the ability to remain connected to peace, softness, truth, faith, and presence even while life feels heavy. That requires release. Not release from responsibility.

Release from carrying things in ways that are quietly destroying you. Some burdens are meant to be processed, not permanently stored. Grief must eventually be acknowledged. Disappointment must eventually be named.

Bitterness must eventually be confronted before it transforms into identity. Because bitterness changes the way people experience life. It distorts interpretation. It makes hope feel naive. It turns vulnerability into risk. It creates emotional walls that protect pain while also preventing connection.

And the frightening thing about bitterness is that it often feels justified. People rarely become bitter without reason. But justified pain can still become destructive if left unresolved for too long.

This is why forgiveness is less about excusing others and more about refusing to let unresolved pain permanently occupy your inner life. Forgiveness does not always happen quickly. Sometimes it happens gradually. Quietly. In layers.

Sometimes forgiveness begins simply by admitting: I do not want to carry this forever. That is a sacred beginning. Because what people silently carry eventually shapes the quality of their lives.

The atmosphere of a person's inner world influences everything: their relationships, their decision making, their peace, and their emotional availability. It influences their ability to experience joy, their ability to trust, and their ability to remain open to life again after disappointment.

A Juanderful Life cannot fully grow in an atmosphere weighed down by years of unprocessed emotional heaviness.

Something must be released.

Something must be faced honestly.

Something must finally be allowed to heal.

Healing does not mean forgetting. It means the wound no longer controls the direction of your life. That is different. And healing rarely arrives through pretending nothing hurt. It often begins when someone finally becomes gentle enough with themselves to admit:

I have carried this long enough. Sometimes strength is not continuing to carry everything alone. Sometimes strength is finally setting something down.

Some people have not had a deep breath emotionally in years. Not a real one. Not the kind that reaches the deepest parts of the body and reminds you that you are safe enough to unclench.

Many people move through life carrying invisible tension they no longer even recognize. Their shoulders remain tight. Their thoughts never fully quiet. Even moments of rest feel temporary because internally, they are still bracing for the next demand, the next disappointment, the next problem requiring their attention.

Over time, constant emotional bracing begins to feel normal. People laugh while exhausted. Show up while depleted. Encourage others while privately unraveling. And because they continue functioning, no one realizes how much weight they are actually carrying. Sometimes not even them.

Release sometimes begins with something almost embarrassingly small. A deeper breath. Five quiet minutes before reaching for the phone in the morning. Sitting in the car for a moment before walking into the house. Learning to notice tension instead of immediately overriding it. Tiny moments of return matter more than people realize.

Chapter 4

I'M FINE

The Cost of Always Being Fine

There is a cost to always being fine. At first, it may feel like strength. You learn to answer quickly. Smile politely. Keep the conversation moving. You become skilled at giving people the version of you that requires the least explanation. Fine becomes efficient. Fine becomes socially acceptable.

Fine becomes the word you use when the truth feels too heavy, too complicated, or too inconvenient to unfold in the middle of an ordinary day. But over time, always being fine can become a quiet form of self-abandonment.

You stop pausing long enough to ask what you actually feel. You stop expecting anyone to notice the difference between your smile and your weariness. You stop giving language to the places inside you that still ache. Eventually, fine becomes less of an answer and more of a room you keep locking yourself inside. A Juanderful Life demands more honesty than that.

Not with everyone.

Not in every room.

Not at every moment.

But somewhere, somehow, the truth must have a place to breathe. Because what remains unnamed does not remain harmless. It gathers. It settles.

It becomes tension in the body, distance in relationships, heaviness in prayer, impatience in conversations, and exhaustion that sleep alone cannot repair.

Some people are not tired because they are weak. They are tired because they have spent years translating pain into politeness. They have learned how to make discomfort presentable. How to make disappointment sound manageable. How to carry grief without making anyone uncomfortable. And while that may keep life moving, it does not always keep the soul well.

There is a difference between privacy and suppression. Privacy is sacred. Suppression is costly. Privacy says, "I will share my truth with wisdom."

Suppression says, "I will pretend there is no truth to share."

A Juanderful Life honors the difference. It does not demand that you expose every wound or explain every private battle. But it does invite you to stop disappearing behind answers that no longer tell the truth. Sometimes healing begins when "I'm fine" becomes:

I am tired.

I am disappointed.

I am grieving something I have not fully named.

I need time.

I need quiet.

I need help.

I need to stop pretending this has not affected me. Those words may not fix everything immediately. But they open a door. And sometimes the soul does not need a solution first. Sometimes it needs permission to stop performing wellness.

When Strength Becomes a Hiding Place

Strength can become a beautiful thing. It can help you endure what you did not expect. It can steady you when life feels uncertain. It can give you the courage to keep showing up when quitting would be easier. But strength can also become a hiding place. Especially when people begin praising you for never needing anything.

You become the dependable one. The composed one. The one who handles pressure. The one who figures it out.

The one who can be counted on no matter what is happening inside. At first, that identity may feel honorable. And in many ways, it is.

There is dignity in being responsible. There is beauty in being faithful. There is grace in showing up for people you love.

But there is also danger in becoming known only for your capacity. Because when people only see your strength, they may forget to look for your tenderness. They may forget that you need care too. They may assume your silence means ease. They may mistake your endurance for absence of pain. And eventually, you may begin believing it yourself.

You may start thinking that needing support makes you less capable. That admitting exhaustion makes you less faithful. That softness must be earned only after everything else has been handled. But a Juanderful Life cannot be built on constant emotional concealment. It requires a strength that is honest enough to be human. There is a kind of strength that performs. And there is a kind of strength that tells the truth.

Performed strength says:
I can carry it all.

Honest strength says:
I have carried a lot, and I need wisdom about what is still mine to hold.

Performed strength says:
I am fine.

Honest strength says:
I am still standing, but I am also tired.

Performed strength says:
Nothing affects me.

Honest strength says:
This affected me, and I am willing to heal instead of harden.

That kind of strength is quieter. Less impressive to people who only admire endurance. But it is more sustainable. Because no one can live a Juanderful Life while constantly hiding behind the very strength that was meant to help them survive.

Strength should support your life. It should not become the wall that keeps your soul unseen.

Sometimes, the bravest thing a strong person can do is stop pretending they do not need gentleness.

Sometimes courage looks like receiving care without apologizing for needing it.

Sometimes strength becomes truest when it finally allows room for softness.

The Body Carrying What the Mouth Never Said

The body often tells the truth before the mouth is ready.

A tight jaw.

A clenched stomach.

Shoulders that rise without permission.

A chest that feels guarded even in quiet rooms.

Hands that stay busy because stillness feels too revealing.

Many people think silence means something has disappeared. But silence does not always mean release. Sometimes silence simply means the body has become the place where unspoken things are stored.

Words never said.

Tears never given space.

Anger swallowed for the sake of peace.

Grief postponed because life kept requiring function.

Disappointment folded neatly into the background so no one would have to feel uncomfortable.

Over time, what is unspoken can begin to live physically. Not as punishment. As memory. The body remembers what the mind tries to organize quickly.

It remembers pressure.

It remembers shock.

It remembers the moments you had to keep moving when you wanted to collapse.

It remembers the conversations you replayed but never fully processed.

It remembers the times you smiled while something inside you was still aching.

This is why some people feel tired in ways they cannot explain. The exhaustion is not only from what they are doing. Sometimes it is from what they have never been able to say. A Juanderful Life requires listening to the body with compassion.

Not fear.

Not obsession.

Compassion.

Because the body may be carrying messages the heart has not yet found language for.

That headache.

That tightness.

That restlessness.

That inability to settle.

That constant bracing for something to go wrong.

Sometimes these are invitations to pay attention.

To slow down.

To ask, What have I been holding?

What have I been swallowing?

What have I been carrying in silence because I did not know where else to put it?

The goal is not to blame the body. The goal is to honor it as part of your story. Your body has helped you survive seasons your words could not fully explain. It has carried you through days when your spirit felt weary. It has continued breathing, walking, working, holding, and showing up. Even when you did not know how heavy life had become. That deserves tenderness.

Some people need to learn that release is not only emotional.

It can be physical too.

A deeper breath.

A softened jaw.

A moment of stillness without apology.

A walk that lets the body move grief instead of store it.

A prayer whispered with the shoulders finally lowered.

A quiet admission: I have been carrying more than I realized. That admission may not change everything immediately. But it begins something sacred. It begins the return from silent storage to conscious release. And sometimes, the body begins to heal when the truth finally has somewhere else to go.

The Beginning of Release

Release does not always begin with a dramatic breakthrough. Sometimes it begins with a small admission that can open a door that has been closed for years. Many people imagine release as a single emotional moment where everything lifts at once. But often, release is quieter than that. It comes in layers. A little honesty here. A little softness there.

A little more willingness to stop defending the version of yourself that learned to survive by staying guarded.

Release is not forgetting. It is not pretending that something did not matter. It is not excusing what wounded you. It is the slow return of your inner life from the grip of what happened.

A Juanderful Life requires that kind of return. Because what you refuse to release may eventually begin shaping what you believe is possible.

Unreleased disappointment can make hope feel unsafe.

Unreleased resentment can make peace feel unreachable.

Unreleased grief can make joy feel disloyal.

Unreleased fear can make every new beginning feel dangerous.

That is why release is not weakness. It is stewardship of the soul. It is deciding that your inner life deserves care, not just endurance. Sometimes release begins when you stop rehearsing the same pain in your mind.

Sometimes it begins when you tell the truth to God without editing the sentence.

Sometimes it begins when you allow yourself to grieve what you kept minimizing.

Sometimes it begins when you stop waiting for an apology before choosing not to let bitterness build a permanent home inside you.

Release is not always immediate. Some things leave slowly because they entered deeply. That is okay. A Juanderful Life does not demand rushed healing. It invites honest healing.

The kind that makes room for tenderness.

The kind that lets you breathe again.

The kind that helps you stop confusing guardedness with wisdom.

There comes a moment when carrying the pain begins to cost more than facing it. Not because the pain was insignificant. But because your life is too sacred to become a storage place for everything that hurt you. Release begins there.

In the quiet decision that you may still remember what happened, but you will no longer allow it to decide who you become. And sometimes, that decision is the first deep breath the soul has taken in a very long time.

Bridge

From Awareness to Navigation

Awareness is a holy beginning, but it is not the whole journey. There is grace in finally seeing what has been happening beneath the surface. The tilt. The fear. The drift. The weight. The quiet ways a person can keep functioning while something inside them is asking to be noticed.

To see these things clearly is no small matter. Many people live for years without naming what they carry. They adapt to pressure. They normalize exhaustion. They mistake survival for peace and silence for strength. They keep moving because movement feels safer than stillness. But awareness interrupts the pattern.

It brings the hidden thing into the light. It allows a person to say, "This is what happened. This is what I have been carrying. This is where I began to drift. This is where fear changed my sight. This is where I stopped feeling fully present in my own life." That kind of honesty is sacred. But after honesty comes a deeper question.

Now what?

Once you have recognized the tilt, how do you move?

Once you have named the weight, how do you carry life differently?

Once you have seen the drift, how do you choose direction?

This is where navigation begins.

Not as control.

Not as panic.

Not as the pressure to fix everything at once.

Navigation is the quiet wisdom of taking the next faithful step with clearer eyes. A Juanderful Life is not built by awareness alone. It is built when awareness becomes alignment. When truth becomes movement. When the soul stops merely naming what hurts and begins learning how to live with wisdom, faith, and direction.

The next part of this journey is not about rushing forward. It is about learning how to move without losing yourself.

How to make decisions when emotions are loud.

How to know what must be protected.

How to begin before conditions are perfect.

How to remain steady when others depend on you.

Because life will still ask things of you. Even after you become aware.

The phone will still ring.

The bills will still come.

People will still need answers.

The future will still unfold in ways you cannot fully predict. But now, you are not moving blindly.

You are learning to read the moment with wisdom.

You are learning to trust what is steady beneath what is shifting.

You are learning that the horizon is not reached by wishing alone.

It is reached by navigation.

PART II: NAVIGATION

Chapter 5

NAVIGATION

Navigation

There comes a point when seeing what has happened inside you must become movement. Not rushed movement. Not frantic correction. Not the kind of movement born from fear or pressure. But the steady movement of a person who has begun to understand that life cannot be lived well by emotion alone.

Part I was about the tilt. The moment life shifts. The way fear changes sight. The quiet drift away from yourself. The invisible weight people carry.

Part II is about what happens next. Not after everything is fixed. Not after emotions settle perfectly. Not after certainty returns. But in the middle of life as it is. This is where navigation begins.

Navigation is not control. It is attention. It is the quiet discipline of noticing what is true, choosing what is wise, and taking the next faithful step even when your feelings are not yet steady.

A Juanderful Life is not attained by waiting until life becomes calm enough to live well. It is attained by learning how to live awake, aligned, and directed while life is still unfolding.

Reading the Instruments

There are moments when emotions become too loud to be trusted completely. Not because emotions are wrong. Not because they should be ignored. But because emotions, under pressure, do not always tell the whole truth.

Fear may tell you to run. Anger may tell you to speak before wisdom has entered the room. Exhaustion may tell you that everything is impossible. Disappointment may tell you that nothing will ever change.

And in those moments, if you allow emotion to become the only voice guiding your life, you may begin making decisions from the most unstable part of yourself. That is why a centered life requires instruments.

Not physical instruments.

Inner ones.

Practices.

Rhythms.

Truths.

Faith.

Stillness.

Wise counsel.

Prayer.

The small structures that help you find direction when your emotions are shifting too quickly to lead. Every person needs something deeper than mood to live by.

Mood changes with sleep, pressure, disappointment, hunger, weather, memory, conflict, and fear. Mood can rise in the morning and collapse by evening. Mood can be tender one moment and defensive the next.

A life guided only by mood becomes difficult to trust. You may start and stop too often. Open and close too quickly. Speak and regret. Commit and withdraw. Believe and doubt. Not because you lack sincerity, but because your inner weather keeps becoming your compass.

A Juanderful Life requires something steadier. It requires the ability to pause and ask:

What is true beneath what I feel?

What is wise beyond what I want in this moment?

What choice will still honor my peace when this emotion passes?

That kind of questioning is not cold. It is caring. It protects the future from being shaped by a temporary storm inside the present. Some people think discipline means denying emotion. But real discipline is not denial. It is devotion.

Devotion to the life you are trying to build.

Devotion to the peace you are learning to protect.

Devotion to the person you are becoming.

Devotion to the purpose that cannot be governed by every passing feeling.

There will be days when you do not feel clear. Days when prayer feels quiet. Days when your confidence feels thin. Days when you want to retreat from everything that requires courage. Those days do not mean you have failed. They mean you need instruments.

A simple routine.

A moment of silence before responding.

A trusted voice that helps you hear beyond fear.

A prayer spoken honestly, even if all you can say is, “God, steady me.”

Sometimes structure is what carries you when strength feels unavailable. And there is grace in that.

A Juanderful Life is not built by always feeling inspired. It is built by having enough sacred structure to keep you aligned when inspiration disappears.

Because feelings are real. But they are not always reliable. And wisdom often begins when you learn to honor what you feel without handing it the wheel.

Lifeboat Decisions

There are seasons when life quietly asks a question most people would rather avoid:

What cannot come with you?

Not because it has no value.

Not because it never mattered.

But because capacity is real.

Every person has limits, even the strong ones. Time has limits. Energy has limits. Attention has limits. Peace has limits when it is constantly spent without being restored.

Much of adulthood is learning that love does not remove limits. Responsibility does not remove limits. Faith does not remove limits. Purpose does not remove limits. A Juanderful Life honors capacity.

Choosing Capacity Over Chaos

One of the clearest signs of wisdom is knowing the difference between what is possible and what is sustainable.

Many people build chaotic lives because they keep saying yes to what they technically can do, without asking whether they have the capacity to carry it well.

There is a difference.

Possible asks, "Can I fit this in?"

Capacity asks, "Can I carry this without losing myself?"

Possible looks at the calendar.

Capacity looks at the whole person.

Your energy.

Your peace.

Your family.

Your health.

Your faith.

Your emotional reserves.

Your ability to be present and not merely productive.

Chaos often begins when people ignore capacity. They keep adding responsibilities, relationships, projects, expectations, and emotional burdens until life becomes crowded with things that may be good individually but destructive collectively.

Not every good thing belongs in this season.

Not every request is an assignment.

Not every open door is a door you are supposed to walk through.

A Juanderful Life requires discernment about capacity. It asks you to stop measuring strength by how much you can hold and begin measuring wisdom by what you know to release.

This is not weakness.

This is stewardship.

You cannot protect peace while constantly overloading your life. You cannot live awake while rushing from one demand to another. You cannot hear God clearly if every quiet space is filled with noise, obligation, and exhaustion. Capacity is not just about time.

It is about inner room.

Room to think.

Room to pray.

Room to breathe.

Room to recover.

Room to love without resentment.

Room to make decisions without panic.

Room to live as a whole person, not a constantly available one.

Chaos will always ask for more.

More attention.

More reaction.

More urgency.

More emotional energy.

More explanation.

More proving.

But capacity asks a better question: What can I carry faithfully in this season? That question can save a life from becoming overcrowded.

Sometimes choosing capacity means disappointing someone.

Sometimes it means delaying something.

Sometimes it means admitting that what once fit no longer fits.

Sometimes it means releasing the version of yourself that needed to be everything to everybody. That release can feel uncomfortable at first, especially for people who are used to being dependable. But dependability without boundaries eventually becomes depletion. A life of alignment does not glorify depletion. It honors wisdom.

It understands that peace must have space. Purpose must have space. Faith must have space. Healing must have space. Joy must have space.

If everything is urgent, nothing is sacred.

If everything has access to you, nothing is protected.

If every request receives your yes, your life may eventually lose the shape of your calling. Choosing capacity over chaos means becoming honest about the limits that protect your life.

It means saying:

This matters, but I cannot carry it right now.

I care, but I cannot be consumed.

I can help, but I cannot abandon myself.

I can build, but not at the cost of my peace.

I can love, but I cannot control every outcome.

Those are not selfish statements. They are mature ones. A Juanderful Life is not a life where you carry everything. It is a life where you carry what is yours with faith, wisdom, and enough peace to remain whole while you do it.

Chapter 6

READINESS

The Myth of Perfect Conditions

Most people are not waiting because they lack desire. They are waiting because they want certainty first. They want the timing to feel right. They want the money to be settled. They want the fear to disappear.

They want the plan to make complete sense before they take the first step. But life rarely becomes perfectly arranged before it asks us to move.

There is almost always something unfinished. Something unclear. Something inconvenient. Something that makes obedience, growth, or change feel slightly unreasonable. That is why perfect conditions can become one of the most convincing forms of delay.

It sounds wise.

It sounds patient.

It sounds responsible.

But sometimes what we call waiting is really fear wearing mature language. A Juanderful Life is not built by waiting until every uncertainty disappears. It is built by learning how to move with wisdom while some things are still unresolved.

This does not mean rushing. It does not mean forcing doors open. It does not mean ignoring timing, counsel, prayer, or preparation. It means understanding that preparation and hesitation are not the same thing.

Preparation strengthens movement.

Hesitation postpones it.

Preparation gathers what is needed.

Hesitation keeps moving the starting line.

Preparation asks, What is the next wise step?

Hesitation asks, What if I fail?

There is a difference. Many people lose years waiting for a version of life that never arrives. They imagine a future moment when they will finally feel ready enough to begin. Ready to write, to heal, or to forgive. Ready to build, to rest, or to change. Ready to live with more intention.

But readiness is often misunderstood. Sometimes readiness does not feel like confidence. Sometimes it feels like quiet willingness. A willingness to begin small. A willingness to be imperfect. A willingness to learn while moving. A willingness to trust that clarity may come after the first step, not before it.

Some doors do not open from a distance. They open as you approach them. That is difficult for people who want guarantees before movement. It requires faith. It requires humility. It requires the acceptance that you may not know everything at the beginning and still be called to begin.

A balanced existence does not demand perfect visibility. It requires enough light for the next faithful step. That step may not impress anyone. It may not look dramatic. It may not feel powerful.

But small movement matters when fear has convinced you to stay still. Sometimes the next step is making the appointment.

Writing the first page.

Having the conversation.

Creating the plan.

Returning to prayer.

Cleaning the room.

Opening the document.

Taking the walk.

Saying yes.

Saying no.

Starting again.

Not because everything is perfect.

Because your life is still asking to be lived.

There is a quiet grief in waiting too long. Not the grief of one obvious loss, but the grief of unused possibility. The ache of knowing you kept postponing what mattered because you were waiting to feel less afraid.

Fear rarely disappears before movement. Often, it loosens as movement begins. You take one step and realize you did not fall apart.

You take another and realize you are stronger than the story fear told you. You keep going and discover that courage was not waiting for fear to leave. Courage was learning to move with fear present, but not in charge.

This is one of the great shifts in a Juanderful Life. You stop treating discomfort as a stop sign.

You begin asking whether discomfort is actually part of the invitation.

Some growth feels uncomfortable because it is wrong. But some growth feels uncomfortable because it is new. Discernment is learning the difference.

Newness can feel unsafe simply because it is unfamiliar. Peace can feel strange after years of pressure. Rest can feel unproductive when you have measured worth by output. A healthier rhythm can feel awkward when chaos has been normal.

That does not mean you are moving in the wrong direction. It may mean you are learning a new way to live. Perfect conditions are often less important than honest alignment.

Is this step aligned with peace?

Is it aligned with purpose?

Is it aligned with faith?

Is it aligned with the person I am becoming?

If the answer is yes, then the absence of perfect conditions should not automatically become permission to delay. There will always be reasons to wait. Always, another bill, another responsibility, another fear. But a life cannot be lived only in preparation.

At some point, preparation must become participation.

At some point, the dream must become a decision.

At some point, healing must become more than something you hope for.

At some point, faith must move from belief into step.

This does not require grand gestures.

In fact, most meaningful change begins quietly.

A small act repeated.

A boundary honored.

A habit restored.

A truth admitted.

A beginning protected.

A decision made without applause.

These are the hidden movements that change a life. A Juanderful Life is not waiting somewhere beyond perfect circumstances. It is being formed in the choices you make while circumstances are still imperfect.

The question is not, " When will everything be ready?"

The deeper question is, what can I do faithfully with what I have now? That question returns power to the present. It reminds you that you do not need the whole future in your hands to take responsibility for this day.

You do not need perfect confidence to begin.

You do not need perfect peace to choose wisely.

You do not need perfect timing to take one honest step.

You only need enough willingness to stop letting imperfection become the reason you never move. Because sometimes the life you are praying for is waiting on the other side of the step you keep postponing.

Staying Steady When Others Depend on You

There is a particular kind of pressure that comes when other people are watching how you respond.

Not watching with criticism necessarily.

Sometimes watching with need.

A child looking for reassurance.

A spouse listening for steadiness in your voice.

A team waiting to see whether you are worried.

A family quietly measuring the room by your reaction.

A client, a friend, a congregation, a business, a household, all needing something from you while you are still trying to gather yourself inside. This kind of moment asks something different from a person.

It asks for steadiness.

Not perfection.

Not emotional numbness.

Not pretending nothing is wrong.

Steadiness.

The ability to remain present enough that your fear does not become the atmosphere everyone else has to breathe.

That is not easy.

Especially when you are carrying your own questions.

Especially when you are tired.

Especially when you wish someone would look at you and say, "You do not have to be strong right now."

But life often places people in positions where they must comfort others while still needing comfort themselves. That is one of the quiet burdens of responsibility.

You may be the one others look to because you have been dependable before. Because you usually know what to do. Because you have learned how to keep moving when things become difficult. Because somewhere along the way, people began associating your presence with safety.

That can be beautiful.

It can also be heavy.

A Juanderful Life does not require you to deny the weight of being needed. It asks you to carry that responsibility with truth.

There is a difference between steady leadership and silent suffering. Steady leadership says, "I may not have every answer, but I will not add chaos to the room."

Silent suffering says, "I must hide everything I feel so no one else becomes uncomfortable." One creates safety. The other creates isolation.

Many people confuse the two. They believe staying steady means never admitting concern, never needing help, never showing emotion, never pausing long enough to breathe. But real steadiness is not the absence of feeling. It is the presence of being grounded. It is the quiet discipline of choosing your tone carefully.

Choosing your timing wisely.

Choosing not to transfer your panic onto people who are already afraid.

Choosing not to make permanent declarations from temporary pressure.

Choosing not to let the loudest emotion in the room become the leader.

Sometimes steadiness sounds simple.

“We are going to take this one step at a time.”

“I do not know everything yet, but I know what we can do next.”

“Let us not solve the whole future today.”

“We will face what is in front of us with wisdom.”

Those sentences may not fix the situation. But they can lower the temperature of the room.

And sometimes lowering the temperature is the first act of care.

People do not always need you to have instant solutions. Sometimes they need your nervous system not to become another emergency. They need to feel that someone is still present.

Still listening.

Still discerning.

Still able to hold the moment without making it heavier.

This is sacred work.

It happens in homes more than boardrooms.

In kitchens.

In cars.

In waiting rooms.

In late night conversations.

In the pause before you answer a difficult question.

In the breath you take before responding to bad news.

In the decision to speak from wisdom instead of woundedness.

What you carry inwardly eventually enters your language, your tone, your patience, your decisions, and the atmosphere you create around you. This is why inner connectivity matters. Not because you are responsible for everyone's emotions. You are not.

When people depend on you, your steadiness can become a shelter while they find their own. That does not mean you become the savior. It means you become anchored enough not to make the storm worse. There is humility in that. Because staying steady does not mean you always feel strong.

Sometimes it means you step away for a moment and pray before you speak.

Sometimes it means you say less because your first response would not be your wisest one.

Sometimes it means you admit, "I need a minute."

Sometimes it means you ask for help instead of quietly resenting everyone who needs you.

Sometimes it means you stop confusing availability with love.

People who depend on you do not need access to every unprocessed emotion. But they do need access to your honesty. Healthy steadiness does not pretend. It communicates with care. It tells the truth without flooding the room. It gives enough information to create clarity without using fear as a weapon. It honors reality without surrendering hope.

This is where faith becomes more than language. Faith becomes posture. Not a performance of certainty, but a way of standing when certainty is incomplete.

Faith steadies the part of you that wants to collapse into every possible outcome. It reminds you that you are not holding the entire future alone.

It gives you permission to lead the next moment without pretending you control the whole story. That matters when others depend on you.

Because dependence can tempt you to believe you must be everything.

The answer.

The shield.

The provider.

The comforter.

The strategist.

The emotional container.

The one who never breaks rhythm.

But no human being can become everything without losing something sacred. A Juanderful Life requires a steadiness that includes surrender.

You can be responsible without being consumed.

You can be dependable without being depleted.

You can be strong without becoming unreachable.

You can lead without pretending you never need to be led.

That is a mature kind of steadiness.

The kind that does not collapse under need.

The kind that does not harden under pressure.

The kind that remains human.

Sometimes the people who depend on you need to see that steadiness and humanity can exist together. They need to know that courage can have tears in its eyes.

That wisdom can pause.

That faith can ask questions.

That strength can receive support.

That leadership can breathe.

This is how a Juanderful Life becomes visible to others. Not through perfection. Through presence. Through the way you enter difficult rooms without surrendering your peace.

Through the way you tell the truth without spreading fear.

Through the way you keep your heart soft while carrying real responsibility.

Through the way you remember that being needed is not the same as being owned.

There will be seasons when others depend on you heavily.

When your voice matters.

When your calm matters.

When your choices shape more than your own day. In those seasons, do not confuse steadiness with silence. Do not confuse responsibility with self-abandonment.

Do not confuse leadership with loneliness. You are allowed to be supported while supporting others. You are allowed to breathe while others are waiting.

You are allowed to be honest while remaining steady. And sometimes the most powerful thing you can offer is not a perfect answer. It is a grounded presence. A quiet assurance. A faithful next step. A reminder that even here, even now, life can still be navigated with wisdom.

Chapter 7

RETURNING TO YOURSELF

Coming Back to the Person Beneath Pressure, Survival, and Performance

There comes a time when the life you have been managing begins asking for something deeper than management. It asks for return. Not return to who you were before life became complicated. Not return to innocence.

Not return to a version of yourself untouched by disappointment, pressure, grief, responsibility, or change. That person may no longer exist in the same way.

Life has taught you things. Some lessons came gently. Others came through seasons you would not have chosen. You have carried weight. Made decisions. Endured uncertainty. Held yourself together in rooms where no one knew how much it cost you to remain composed.

So, returning to yourself does not mean becoming who you used to be. It means coming back to what is still true beneath everything you had to survive. The quiet self. The honest self.

The self that still knows what peace feels like, even if peace has been distant. The self that remembers joy without needing permission. The self that can hear God without all the noise of fear, performance, and constant proving.

Sometimes people lose themselves slowly. Not because they are careless. Because life becomes demanding.

Responsibilities grow.

Expectations multiply.

People need things.

Bills need paying.

Families need tending.

Businesses need decisions.

Dreams need attention.

Pain needs somewhere to go.

And somewhere in the middle of all that motion, a person can begin living from function instead of fullness.

They keep showing up.

Keep producing.

Keep answering.

Keep smiling.

Keep carrying.

But inwardly, something becomes quiet.

Not peaceful quiet.

Absent quiet.

The kind of quiet that comes when a person has stopped asking, "What do I need?" because the answer feels inconvenient.

A Juanderful Life cannot be built only from what the world requires of you. It must also be built from what keeps you whole. That is why return matters.

Return is the sacred act of noticing where you have been absent from your own life. It may begin in a small moment.

You sit in your car after a long day and realize you do not want to rush inside yet. You stand in the kitchen and feel the weight of everything you have not said.

You wake up tired, not only in your body, but somewhere deeper. You hear yourself laugh and realize you have missed that sound.

You pray and notice that your words have become routine, but your heart is asking for something real.

These moments are not failures.

They are invitations.

They are the soul whispering, "Come back."

Come back from constant proving.

Come back from performing strength.

Come back from living only in response to what others need.

Come back from the version of yourself that learned to survive by staying busy, guarded, and useful. Survival can be necessary for a season. But survival was never meant to become your permanent identity.

There is a difference between surviving a season and becoming shaped entirely by survival. When survival becomes identity, rest feels suspicious.

Softness feels unsafe.

Joy feels irresponsible.

Peace feels temporary.

You begin preparing for loss even when nothing has happened.

You begin managing every room instead of inhabiting it.

You begin confusing control with safety. And slowly, without meaning to, you become loyal to the very tension that exhausted you. Returning to yourself means telling the truth about that.

It means admitting that some patterns protected you once, but they may now be keeping you from living freely. The guardedness. The overthinking.

The need to anticipate every possible problem. The habit of carrying more than your share.

The instinct to say "I'm fine" before you have even asked yourself whether it is true. These things may have helped you make it through. But making it through is not the same as being fully alive.

A Juanderful Life asks for more than endurance. It asks for presence. It asks you to become available to your own life again. Not just available to responsibility.

Available to beauty.

Available to stillness.

Available to laughter.

Available to prayer.

Available to rest.

Available to love that does not require you to earn it through exhaustion. That kind of availability can feel unfamiliar at first. Especially if you have spent years being needed.

Being needed can become a powerful identity. It can make you feel valuable. Important. Necessary. But being needed is not the same as being nourished.

A person can be needed by many and still feel unseen. A person can be respected and still feel lonely.

A person can be praised for strength and still be longing for a place where they do not have to explain why they are tired. Return begins when you stop confusing usefulness with wholeness.

You are more than what you can carry.

More than what you can fix.

More than what you can produce.

More than what others expect from you.

More than the role you play in every room.

There is a self beneath the roles.

A self, God still sees clearly.

A self that has not disappeared, even if life has buried it beneath pressure.

Returning to yourself is not selfish. It is stewardship. You cannot keep pouring from a place you refuse to tend.

You cannot keep calling yourself strong while ignoring the parts of you that are asking for care.

You cannot build a Juanderful Life while abandoning the inner life that gives everything else meaning.

Sometimes return looks like rest.

Sometimes it looks like honesty.

Sometimes it looks like changing your pace.

Sometimes it looks like letting silence tell you what noise has been covering.

Sometimes it looks like saying no without writing a long explanation.

Sometimes it looks like saying yes to something that restores you.

Sometimes it looks like grieving what you kept minimizing.

Sometimes it looks like remembering that God never asked you to become unreachable to be faithful.

There is grace in return. You do not have to come back to yourself all at once. You can begin with one honest breath.

One quiet prayer.

One truthful sentence.

One moment where you stop performing wellness and simply admit, "I am here, and I want to live awake again."

That is enough for a beginning.

A Juanderful Life is not found by escaping every demand. It is found by refusing to let demands erase your soul. It is found when you learn to live with responsibility without losing tenderness.

With ambition without losing peace.

With faith without pretending.

With strength without hiding.

With purpose without abandoning presence.

Returning to Yourself

Returning to yourself is not the end of the journey. It is the beginning of living from a truer place. Because beneath the pressure, beneath survival, beneath performance, beneath all the versions of yourself you became to make it through, something sacred remains. You are still there. And the life ahead is asking you to keep going. It is asking you to come home to yourself while you go.

Returning to yourself is not always dramatic. Sometimes it begins quietly. You notice that you are tired before you explain it away. You admit that something no longer feels aligned. You stop calling every discomfort "just a season." You allow yourself to tell the truth without immediately turning the truth into a task. That is often where return begins.

Not with a grand announcement. Not with a complete life change. But with one honest moment where you stop abandoning yourself for the sake of appearing fine.

Many people think returning to themselves means going back to who they used to be. But sometimes the old version of you cannot hold the wisdom of what you have survived. Return is not regression. It is reconnection.

It is coming back to the truest parts of yourself after life, pressure, grief, responsibility, and survival have pulled you away from them.

You may not return as the same person. You may return softer in some places and stronger in others. More discerning. Less willing to perform peace while privately living in tension. More aware of what drains you. More protective of what restores you.

A Juanderful Life makes room for that kind of return. It gives you permission to become honest without becoming harsh.

To change without calling yourself inconsistent.

To rest without calling yourself lazy.

To release without calling yourself weak.

Sometimes returning to yourself means remembering what peace feels like.

Sometimes it means praying again with your whole heart instead of your exhausted routine.

Sometimes it means laughing without guilt.

Sometimes it means sitting quietly long enough to hear what your spirit has been trying to say.

The return may be slow.

That is okay.

Some parts of you have waited a long time to be noticed again. You do not have to rush the process of becoming present. You only have to begin. And sometimes beginning sounds like this:

I am still here.

Beneath the pressure.

Beneath the performance.

Beneath the survival.

Beneath all the versions of myself I became, to make it through. I am still here. And I am ready to live awake again

Chapter 8

LEARNING TO LIVE UNBRACED

Releasing Constant Vigilance and Learning to Receive Peace Again

Some people do not know they are bracing until life finally becomes quiet.

The room settles.

The phone stops ringing.

No one is asking a question.

No immediate problem is demanding an answer.

And yet the body remains prepared.

The shoulders stay lifted.

The jaw stays tight.

The breath stays shallow. The mind keeps scanning for what might happen next. That is the strange exhaustion of living braced.

Even when the moment is safe, something inside you is still waiting for impact. Constant vigilance can become so familiar that peace feels suspicious. Instead of receiving quiet as a gift, you begin treating it as a pause before the next problem. You do not rest fully because some part of you believes rest will make you unprepared. You do not soften completely because softness feels like exposure.

So, you remain ready.

Ready for disappointment.

Ready for conflict.

Ready for bad news.

Ready for someone to need you.

Ready for life to shift again.

At first, bracing may have been necessary. There are seasons when people learn to protect themselves because life has been unpredictable. They learn to think ahead, anticipate needs, prepare for outcomes, and stay emotionally alert because something important once depended on it. Bracing can begin as wisdom. But if it never relaxes, it becomes a prison.

A Juanderful Life cannot fully grow in a body and spirit that are always preparing for danger. It needs room to breathe. Room to trust. Room to receive what is good without immediately questioning how long it will last.

Living unbraced does not mean living carelessly. It does not mean ignoring reality.

It does not mean pretending pain never happened or that life will never become difficult again.

It means learning that you do not have to meet every ordinary moment as though it is an emergency. It means allowing peace to be real while it is here.

Many people say they want peace, but when peace arrives, they do not know how to receive it. So, they fill the silence by creating another task, checking another message, or revisiting another worry. They search for something to solve. Not because they enjoy chaos, but because chaos has become familiar. And familiar things can feel safer than healing at first.

Peace requires a different kind of courage. The courage to stop rehearsing disaster. The courage to let your body believe that this moment does not require defense.

The courage to trust that you can be responsible without being tense. The courage to believe that softness will not make you weak.

There is a difference between being prepared and being perpetually guarded.

Preparation says, “I will be wise.”

Guardedness says, “I cannot afford to relax.”

Preparation gives you structure.

Guardedness steals your breath.

Preparation helps you respond.

Guardedness keeps you living in reaction to things that have not happened yet.

A well-navigated life knows the difference. It understands that vigilance may help you survive a difficult season, but presence helps you live after it.

Some people have survived so much that their nervous system has mistaken tension for loyalty. They feel guilty when they are not worried. They feel irresponsible when they are not carrying something. They feel exposed when they are not managing the emotional temperature of every room.

But worry is not proof of love. Tension is not proof of responsibility. Exhaustion is not proof of faithfulness. You can care deeply and still breathe. You can love people and still rest.

You can be responsible and still allow peace to enter your life without apology. Learning to live unbraced often begins in small ways.

Noticing when your shoulders rise.

Letting your breath deepen before you answer.

Allowing silence to remain silent.

Sitting with joy without preparing for it to be taken.

Receiving help without explaining why you deserve it.

Letting a peaceful day be peaceful.

These may seem small, but for someone who has lived guarded for years, they are sacred acts of return.

A Juanderful Life asks you to stop treating peace like something you must earn after everything else is handled. Peace is not only a reward at the end of pressure. Sometimes peace is the strength that helps you move through pressure without losing yourself.

There will always be something unfinished. Always something uncertain. Always something that could become a concern.

If you wait until every possible problem disappears before you allow yourself to breathe, you may spend your life postponing peace.

Living unbraced means accepting that peace can exist beside unfinished things. You can have unanswered questions and still be held.

You can have responsibilities and still be restored. You can have memories of hard seasons and still allow today to be gentle. This is not denial. It is healing.

Healing teaches the body that the past is not always repeating. Healing teaches the heart that caution does not have to become captivity. Healing teaches the soul that God can be trusted not only in crisis, but also in calm.

Sometimes calm is where trust is tested most. Because in crisis, you know you need God. In calm, you must learn to receive without fear.

To stop gripping.

To stop scanning.

To stop assuming that peace is temporary just because pain once interrupted it.

A Juanderful Life makes room for that kind of receiving. It allows you to live with open hands again. Not careless hands. Open hands.

Hands that can hold responsibility without clenching around it.

Hands that can release what is not yours.

Hands that can receive beauty, help, love, rest, and joy without suspicion.

You may not unbrace all at once. Most people do not. The body may need time. The heart may need reassurance. The mind may need practice. That is okay. You are not failing because peace feels unfamiliar. You are learning a new posture.

One breath at a time.

One quiet moment at a time.

One honest surrender at a time.

And perhaps this is one of the gentlest truths of a Juanderful Life: You do not have to remain tense to remain strong. You do not have to stay guarded to stay wise.

You do not have to keep bracing for impact in order to prove that you survived. Sometimes the next chapter of your life begins when your soul finally realizes it is allowed to exhale.

Bridge

From Navigation to Return

Navigation teaches you how to move. But return teaches you how to live from a restored place.

There is wisdom in learning how to make decisions when emotions are loud. There is strength in knowing what must be protected, what must be released, and what cannot continue receiving access to your peace. There is courage in moving before conditions are perfect and steadiness in remaining grounded when others depend on you.

These are necessary skills. But they are not the final destination. A person can navigate well and still feel far from themselves.

They can make responsible decisions, maintain direction, manage pressure, and keep life moving, while still longing for something quieter and deeper within. Because movement alone does not heal the soul. Direction matters, but so does return.

At some point, the question changes.

Not only, "What should I do next?"

But, "Who am I becoming as I move?"

Not only, "How do I handle this?"

But, "Am I still connected to peace, faith, truth, and the person God is forming within me?"

A Juanderful Life is not merely a well-managed life. It is an aligned life. A life where the outer movement and the inner condition begin to agree. That is why the journey must now turn inward again.

Not backward. Inward.

Toward the places that need rest.

Toward the parts of you that have lived braced for too long.

Toward the peace you kept postponing.

Toward the faith that remained present even when the future was unclear.

The Return is not about abandoning responsibility. It is about refusing to let responsibility erase your spirit. It is the sacred work of coming back to yourself with wisdom.

Coming back to God with honesty.

Coming back to peace without apology.

Coming back to a life that can hold both purpose and tenderness.

Navigation helped you move through uncertainty. Now return helps you become whole as you move. The horizon is found not only by moving forward.

Sometimes it is found by coming home to what is true within you.

PART III: THE RETURN

Chapter 9

THE QUIET DISCIPLINE OF PEACE

Protecting Peace as a Daily Practice, not a Distant Reward

Peace is often treated like something people will reach later.

After the bills are paid.

After the children are settled.

After the business grows.

After the relationship improves.

After the house is quiet.

After the pressure lifts.

After life finally becomes easier to manage.

But if peace is always postponed until everything is finished, most people will spend their lives waiting for a day that never fully arrives. There is almost always something unfinished.

Something uncertain.

Something requiring attention.

Something that could be improved.

Something that needs prayer, patience, wisdom, or work.

If peace depends on the absence of every concern, then peace becomes fragile. It becomes something life can take away too easily. One phone call. One unexpected bill. One hard conversation. One delay. One disappointment.

A Juanderful Life requires a deeper kind of peace. Not peace as escape. Not peace as denial. Not peace as pretending nothing hurts. But peace as a practiced way of living. A quiet discipline.

A daily decision to protect the inner atmosphere of your life from being governed by every demand, fear, opinion, or interruption. That kind of peace does not arrive accidentally. It is cultivated. Protected. Chosen.

Some people think peace should feel effortless if it is real. But often, peace must be practiced precisely because life is not effortless. It must be practiced when the schedule is full, when the answer is delayed, when people misunderstand, when responsibilities are heavy, when the future is still unclear.

Peace is not the absence of pressure. It is the presence of structure beneath pressure. It is the quiet knowing that you can face what is in front of you without surrendering your entire inner world to it.

That does not mean you never feel anxious. It does not mean you never cry. It does not mean your voice never trembles. It means you learn how to return.

Return to breath.

Return to prayer.

Return to truth.

Return to what God has already carried you through.

Return to the present moment instead of letting fear drag you into every possible future at once. The discipline of peace begins with noticing what keeps stealing it.

Not every interruption deserves your whole spirit.

Not every opinion deserves a home in your mind.

Not every conflict requires immediate access to your emotional center.

Not every urgent thing is sacred.

Some things are simply loud. And loud things can train people to live reactively if they are not careful. A life of mastery learns to ask:

Does this deserve my peace?

Does this require my response right now?

Am I being called to act, or am I being pulled into panic? That pause matters. Because peace is often lost in the space between stimulus and reaction.

Someone says something sharp, and you answer from injury. A problem appears, and you immediately imagine disaster. A delay happens, and you begin questioning the entire path. A person disappoints you, and you allow one moment to rewrite the whole relationship.

Peace is protected when you stop letting every external event become an internal emergency. This is not emotional coldness. It is stewardship.

Your inner life is sacred. It should not be left unlocked for every fear, frustration, demand, or distraction to enter freely.

Some doors must be guarded.

The door to your thoughts.

The door to your rest.

The door to your prayer life.

The door to your joy.

The door to your ability to remain soft without becoming easily shaken.

A Juanderful Life requires that kind of guarding. Not guardedness that shuts people out. But discernment that protects what keeps you whole. There is a difference between building walls and keeping watch.

Walls isolate.

Watchfulness preserves.

Walls say, "Nothing can reach me."

Watchfulness says, "Not everything gets to rule me."

That distinction matters.

Because peace is not passivity.

Peace is strength under holy order.

It is the ability to choose your response instead of being dragged by every emotion.

It is the ability to hold concern without becoming consumed.

It is the ability to care deeply without carrying everything destructively.

Some people lose peace because they believe worry proves love.

They worry over their children.

Worry over their business.

Worry over their future.

Worry over people they cannot control.

Worry over outcomes they cannot force.

And because the worry is attached to something meaningful, they begin to confuse anxiety with devotion. But worry is not the same as love. Worry is not the same as wisdom. Worry is not the same as prayer.

You can care deeply without letting fear become the language of your care. You can be responsible without rehearsing every worst-case scenario. You can love people without trying to emotionally control every outcome of their lives.

This is difficult for people who are used to carrying much. They may not know who they are without something to solve.

Quiet may feel unproductive.

Rest may feel undeserved.

Peace may feel almost suspicious.

But peace is not laziness.

Peace is not indifference.

Peace is not the absence of ambition.

Peace is the ground from which a healthier life can be built.

Without peace, ambition becomes frantic. Love becomes anxious. Responsibility becomes resentment. Faith becomes performance. Even success can begin to feel hollow when the inner life is constantly unsettled.

That is why peace must be practiced daily. Not as a reward after life becomes perfect. As a rhythm inside an imperfect life. A moment of stillness before the day begins.

A decision not to check every message immediately.

A prayer before responding.

A boundary around conversations that drain more than they heal.

A refusal to rehearse fear as though it is preparation.

A willingness to let some things wait without calling yourself irresponsible.

Small acts of peace matter. They teach the body that urgency is not always authority. They teach the mind that every thought does not need to be followed. They teach the spirit that God can be trusted in unfinished places.

A Juanderful Life is not a life where nothing disturbs you. It is a life where disturbance no longer owns you. You may still be interrupted. You may still be challenged. You may still face hard news, difficult people, uncertain seasons, and unanswered questions. But you begin to carry them differently.

Less clenched.

Less frantic.

Less surrendered to fear.

Peace becomes not something you visit occasionally, but somewhere inside you learn to live. And when peace becomes a discipline, it also becomes a witness. People may not know exactly what has changed in you, but they feel it.

Your words become slower.

Your presence becomes steadier.

Your decisions become clearer.

Your spirit becomes less easily pulled into every storm around you. That is not because life stopped being difficult. It is because you stopped giving difficulty unlimited access to your inner world. There is power in that. Quiet power.

The kind that does not need to announce itself.

The kind that changes the atmosphere of a room without demanding attention.

The kind that allows you to remain tender without being tossed.

Peace is worth protecting. Not because your life is small. Because your life is sacred. And sacred things require care. So, protect your peace in ordinary ways.

Protect it in the morning.

Protect it in conversation.

Protect it when fear starts narrating the future.

Protect it when old patterns invite you back into panic.

Protect it when the world tries to convince you that constant agitation is normal.

Peace is not a distant reward.

It is a daily practice.

A holy discipline.

A quiet return.

And sometimes, the most powerful evidence of growth is not that life has become easier. It is that your spirit no longer has to leave itself every time life becomes hard.

Chapter 10

FAITH WHEN THE FUTURE IS STILL FORMING

Trusting God While the Full Picture Is Not Yet Visible

Faith is often easiest to talk about after the story makes sense.

After the answer comes.

After the door opens.

After the pain has softened enough to explain.

After the lesson can be named.

After hindsight has arranged the pieces into something understandable.

But the deepest kind of faith is usually formed before clarity arrives.

Before the outcome is visible.

Before the prayer has an answer.

Before the next step feels certain.

Before the future has finished taking shape. That is where faith becomes more than language. It becomes posture.

A way of standing when life has not yet explained itself.

A way of breathing when the next chapter is still unwritten.

A way of trusting God without demanding that He reveal every detail before you obey, rest, or keep going. This is not easy.

There are seasons when the future feels unfinished in every direction. You know something is changing, but you do not know what it will become.

You sense that God is moving, but you cannot yet see how. You feel the discomfort of transition, but not the comfort of arrival. You are no longer where you were, but you are not yet where you are going.

That middle place can feel unsettling. It can make even strong people question themselves.

Did I hear correctly?

Did I move too soon?

Did I wait too long?

Is this delay protection, preparation, or redirection?

Faith does not always answer those questions immediately. Sometimes faith simply keeps you from becoming ruled by them.

A Juanderful Life requires the ability to live faithfully while the picture is still forming. Not because uncertainty feels good. But because uncertainty is part of every meaningful life.

No one receives the full map at the beginning. Most of us receive enough light for the next step. Enough grace for the present moment. Enough strength for today. Enough wisdom to keep from surrendering our peace to what we cannot yet see.

Faith teaches the soul to stop confusing unseen with absent. Just because you cannot see what God is doing does not mean nothing is happening. Seeds grow underground before they break the surface.

Healing begins inwardly before it becomes visible outwardly. Wisdom forms quietly before it becomes language. Direction often develops in hidden places before it becomes a clear path. This is why waiting can feel so difficult.

Waiting is not empty.

Waiting is full of unseen formation.

It is where patience is stretched.

Motives are refined.

Desires are examined.

Trust is tested.

Peace is practiced.

The heart learns whether it only trusts God for outcomes or whether it can trust Him in the process. That is a sacred question.

Can I trust God before I understand?

Can I remain faithful before I feel certain?

Can I keep my heart soft before the answer comes?

Can I believe that my life is still held even when my future is still forming?

These are not small questions. They reach into the deepest places of a person. Because uncertainty has a way of revealing what we have been leaning on.

Control.

Approval.

Timing.

Predictability.

Visible progress.

The reassurance of knowing what comes next.

When those things are removed, faith becomes more honest. Not more polished. More honest.

Sometimes faith sounds like worship.

Sometimes it sounds like weeping.

Sometimes it sounds like silence.

Sometimes it sounds like one tired prayer whispered at the edge of a long day. God, I do not see it yet, but I still trust You.

That prayer may not change the circumstance immediately. But it can change the atmosphere inside you. It can remind your spirit that you are not abandoned in the unfinished place.

It can steady the part of you that wants to rush ahead, force an answer, or build a conclusion from fear. A well-navigated life does not require complete certainty before it chooses peace.

It requires surrender. Not passive surrender. Not the kind that gives up. The kind that releases the illusion that you must understand everything to be held. There is relief in that.

You do not have to carry the full weight of the future in your own hands.

You do not have to solve every possibility tonight.

You do not have to know how every chapter will unfold before you take the next faithful step. Some things are still forming. And forming takes time.

A Juanderful Life makes room for holy process. It does not despise the unfinished places. It does not call every delay denial. It does not assume that hidden work is wasted work. It learns to honor the quiet seasons where God is shaping what cannot yet be seen. This is difficult in a world that celebrates visible progress.

People want announcements. Proof. Results. Evidence that something is happening. But some of the most important work in a life happens before anyone can applaud it.

The healing no one sees.

The obedience no one knows about.

The restraint that kept you from reacting.

The prayer that held you together.

The forgiveness that began privately.

The decision to trust God again after disappointment made trust feel risky. These hidden choices matter. They are part of the forming. They are part of the return. They are part of the life God is building beneath the surface.

Faith when the future is still forming is not about pretending you never wonder. It is about refusing to let wondering become wandering.

You may have questions.

You may have moments when your confidence trembles.

You may need reassurance.

You may need rest.

You may need to admit that waiting is harder than you expected. None of that disqualifies your faith. Faith is not the absence of questions. Faith is the decision to keep turning toward God with the questions still in your hands.

There is tenderness in that. God is not threatened by honest uncertainty. He is not offended by the trembling prayer. He is not distant from the person who says, "I believe, but I am tired."

A Juanderful Life does not require pretending before God. It requires presence with God. The kind of presence that brings the whole self.

The fear.

The hope.

The disappointment.

The longing.

The unfinished dreams.

The fragile trust.

The quiet desire to believe that something beautiful can still be forming even here.

That kind of faith matures a person.

It deepens the roots.

It teaches patience without passivity.

It teaches hope without fantasy.

It teaches surrender without despair.

It teaches movement without panic. And slowly, the person begins to change. Not because everything has become clear. But because they have learned how to remain anchored while clarity is still coming.

That is one of the marks of a Juanderful Life. Not a life where every answer arrives quickly. Not a life where faith removes every uncertainty. But a life where uncertainty no longer has permission to separate you from peace, or God.

There will be times when the future feels like a room still being prepared. You cannot enter it yet. You cannot fully describe it. You may only sense that something is being arranged beyond what you can see.

In those seasons, do not despise the waiting. Do not mistake silence for absence. Do not assume that because the picture is incomplete, the Painter has stopped working. Keep showing up. Keep praying honestly.

Keep taking the next faithful step. Keep protecting your peace. Keep allowing God to form what your eyes cannot yet measure. The future may not be fully visible. But that does not mean it is empty.

Something may be growing. Something may be healing. Something may be aligning.

Something may be preparing you for a life that requires the hope this season is forming. And sometimes, the most sacred thing you can do is trust God in the middle of the unfinished sentence.

Before the period.

Before the answer.

Before the full picture.

Before the horizon becomes clear.

Faith is not only for the arrival. It is for the forming.

Chapter 11

A LIFE THAT FEELS LIKE HOME TO YOUR SPIRIT

Living in Alignment Instead of Performance

There is a kind of life that looks impressive from the outside but feels unfamiliar within. People can admire it. Applaud it. Depend on it. Even envy it.

But the person living it may still feel quietly displaced inside their own existence. That is one of the hidden costs of performance. Performance can build an image while starving the inner life.

It can teach a person how to appear well without actually being well. How to speak with confidence while carrying confusion. How to keep producing while losing tenderness. How to become everything others expect while slowly drifting from what is true.

A Juanderful Life asks for something deeper than appearance. It asks for alignment. This is what happens when the life you are living begins to agree with the truth of who you are becoming.

Your pace agrees with your peace.

Your yes agrees with your values.

Your work agrees with your purpose.

Your relationships agree with your spirit.

Your faith is not something you perform publicly while neglecting privately. Your outer life and inner life begin speaking the same language. That kind of life feels different.

Not perfect.

Not effortless.

But honest.

There is a rest that comes when you stop performing a version of yourself that no longer fits. You no longer have to prove strength in every room.

You no longer have to explain every boundary.

You no longer have to chase every opportunity just because it is available.

You no longer have to confuse being seen with being whole.

A life that feels like home to your spirit is not necessarily quieter on the outside. You may still have responsibilities.

Still have work to do.

Still have people depending on you.

Still have dreams that require discipline.

But inwardly, something settles.

You begin to recognize yourself again.

You begin to move from truth instead of pressure.

You begin to choose what is aligned instead of what is merely impressive. That is a sacred shift. Because performance is exhausting. It requires constant management.

Managing how people see you.

Managing what they expect.

Managing the image.

Managing the applause.

Managing the fear that if you stop producing, proving, or pleasing, someone may decide you are no longer valuable.

You can still build.

Still lead.

Still create.

Still dream.

Still pursue meaningful things.

But you do it from a truer place. Not to convince the world you are enough. But because you are finally living from the life God is forming within you. That is where peace begins to feel less like a visitor and more like an address.

You stop visiting peace only in rare quiet moments. You begin building a life where peace has somewhere to stay. A Juanderful Life is not a life arranged for applause. It is a life arranged around truth. And truth has a way of simplifying what performance made complicated.

Truth helps you see what is no longer yours to carry.

Truth helps you notice when success is costing too much of your soul.

Truth helps you admit when something looks good publicly but feels misaligned privately.

Truth helps you stop calling every open door an assignment.

Not every opportunity belongs to your future.

Not every invitation deserves your yes.

Not every room is worth losing yourself to enter. A life that feels like home to your spirit requires discernment. It asks you to listen beneath noise.

Beneath expectation.

Beneath comparison.

Beneath the fear of disappointing people.

Beneath the old habit of proving. And when you listen long enough, you may discover that your spirit has been telling the truth all along.

This feels heavy.

This feels false.

This feels rushed.

This feels peaceful.

This feels aligned.

This feels like home.

Those inner signals matter.

They are not always loud.

Sometimes they arrive as quiet relief.

A deeper breath.

A softened body.

A clearer mind.

A sense that you do not have to become someone else to belong in the life you are building. That is the beauty of internal order. It does not force you to disappear in order to succeed. It allows you to become more fully present.

More honest.

More grounded.

More available to joy.

More able to love without resentment.

More able to work without losing yourself.

More able to rest without guilt.

There comes a point when a person must decide whether they want a life that impresses others or a life that can actually hold them. Because those are not always the same. Some lives look successful but leave no room for breathing. Some roles bring recognition but require constant self-abandonment.

Some commitments appear noble but quietly drain the very peace they were never meant to cost. A Juanderful Life is not built by ignoring that tension.

It is built by honoring it.

It is built by asking:

Can my spirit live here?

Can my peace survive this pace?

Can my faith remain tender in this environment?

Can my joy breathe inside this commitment?

Can I become who God is calling me to become while continuing to say yes to this?

These questions are not selfish.

They are wise.

Because your life is not only something you manage.

It is something you inhabit.

And if you are going to inhabit it, it should not feel like a place where your spirit is always bracing, shrinking, or apologizing for needing care. It should feel like a place where truth is welcome.

Where peace is protected.

Where purpose has room.

Where faith is nourished.

Where joy is not treated as unnecessary.

Where you can be strong without becoming hidden.

Where you can be useful without being consumed.

Where you can be loved without performing. That is what alignment begins to restore. It gives you back the feeling of being at home within yourself. Not because everything outside you is perfect. But because something inside you is no longer divided.

You are not living one life publicly and another life privately. You are not smiling through what your spirit keeps warning you about. You are not building an image that your inner life cannot survive.

You are learning to live whole. And wholeness is one of the clearest signs of a Juanderful Life. Not a flawless life. A truthful one. A life where your choices increasingly agree with your values. A life where your pace increasingly agrees with your peace.

A life where your ambition increasingly agrees with your purpose. A life where your faith increasingly agrees with your daily rhythm. A life where you do not have to keep abandoning yourself in order to keep everything else standing. That kind of life may require changes. Some gentle. Some difficult. Some long overdue.

But every honest change becomes part of the return. Part of the horizon. Part of the sacred work of living awake. And perhaps that is what many people are really longing for. Not just more success. Not just more recognition. Not just more opportunity. But a life that feels honest to inhabit.

A life where the soul can breathe. A life where peace is not constantly negotiated away. A life where God, purpose, joy, and truth are not squeezed into the margins after everything else has taken priority. A life that feels like home to the spirit. That is not a small thing. That is the horizon coming into view.

Chapter 12

CHOOSING DIRECTION OVER DISTRACTION

Protecting Focus in a Noisy World

The world is loud. Not only with sound. The constant pull of things asking for attention, energy, emotion, and response. A person can wake up with a clear intention and lose it before breakfast. One message can shift the mood. One headline can stir anxiety. One conversation can create doubt. One comparison can make a person question a path they were peaceful about yesterday.

Distraction is not always obvious. Sometimes it does not look like wasting time. Sometimes it looks like chasing too many good things at once. Saying yes too quickly. Listening to too many voices.

Measuring your life against someone else's timeline. Trying to keep up with opportunities that were never assigned to you. Trying to be available everywhere until you are no longer present anywhere. That is the danger of a noisy world.

It does not always pull people toward bad things. Sometimes it pulls them away from the right things. A Juanderful Life requires direction. Not rigid control. Not obsession. Not the refusal to be flexible. Direction.

The quiet inner knowing that your life is moving toward something meaningful, and not every interruption deserves permission to redirect you.

Without direction, distraction becomes powerful. It fills empty space. It borrows your attention. It makes urgency feel like purpose.

It convinces you that movement is the same as progress. But not all movement is progress. Some movement is avoidance. Some movement is reaction. Some movement is comparison dressed up as ambition. Some movement is the fear of being left behind.

An examined life learns to ask a deeper question: Is this taking me toward the life I am called to live, or merely keeping me busy? That question can simplify more than people realize. It can clarify a schedule, expose unnecessary pressure, and create a quiet comparison.

It can help you recognize when your attention has been scattered across things that do not deserve your spirit. Focus is not simply about productivity. It is about devotion. What you focus on receives part of your life. That means focus is sacred. It should not be handed away carelessly.

Many people are tired not because they are doing one hard thing, but because they are giving small pieces of themselves to too many things that do not align with their purpose.

By the end of the day, they feel drained, but they cannot name one single thing that emptied them. That is how distraction works.

It rarely takes everything at once. It takes fragments. And a fragmented life can begin to feel like a life without peace.

A Juanderful Life calls those fragments back. It asks you to become honest about what has been receiving your attention without deserving your devotion.

Not everything needs to come with you into the next season. There is freedom in realizing that you do not have to follow every sound.

Some voices can be heard without being obeyed. Some opportunities can be appreciated without being accepted. Some demands can be acknowledged without being centered.

Some opinions can exist without becoming instructions. The challenge is that distraction often feels easier than direction. Direction requires choice. And choice requires surrender. To choose one path is to release another. To protect one priority is to disappoint another demand.

To honor one's calling is to stop auditioning for every room. That can feel uncomfortable, especially for people who have built an identity around being capable, available, and impressive. But a life cannot become deeply meaningful if it is constantly scattered.

Whatever matters must be protected from whatever merely shouts. A noisy world will not protect your focus for you. It will keep asking. Keep pulling. Keep presenting new reasons to drift. Keep making distractions feel normal.

That is why direction must become a daily choice. Not a dramatic declaration. A daily return to what matters, to what God has placed in your hands.

Return to the work that is yours. Return to the people who need your presence, not just your productivity.

Return to the quiet truth beneath the noise. Sometimes direction looks like turning the phone over. Sometimes it looks like closing the door. Sometimes it looks like finishing what you started before chasing what is new. Sometimes it looks like refusing to let comparison make you despise your own pace. There is a pace that belongs to your life. A rhythm that agrees with your spirit. Your path may not look like everyone else's, but it still carries grace. Distraction often tries to pull you out of that rhythm.

It says you are behind.

You need more.

You should be doing what they are doing.

You should hurry.

You should prove.

You should panic.

But direction answers differently. Direction says:

Stay faithful.

Stay clear.

Stay present.

Stay aligned.

Do not abandon what is sacred because something loud demanded attention. This is one of the quiet marks of a Juanderful Life. The ability to live with intention in a world addicted to interruption.

The ability to keep your eyes on what matters without becoming hard, narrow, or unavailable to beauty. Focus does not mean you stop noticing life. It means you stop letting everything own you.

It means you can enjoy the world without being ruled by it. You can listen without absorbing every opinion. You can serve without becoming scattered. You can build without comparing. You can rest without guilt.

You can move forward without needing everyone to understand the path. A life of direction is not always loud. Often, it is quiet. It is made of private decisions no one applauds. The decision to protect a morning. The decision to pray before reacting. The decision to stop checking what unsettles you. The decision to give your best energy to what is truly yours.

The decision to stop confusing visibility with value. Those choices may seem small, but they shape the atmosphere of a life. They help you become less divided. Less pulled. Less available to every fear. Less dependent on outside noise to tell you who you are. And slowly, your life begins to feel clearer. Not because the world became quiet. But because your direction became stronger.

A Juanderful Life is not found by following every open road. It is formed by walking the path that agrees with your purpose, your peace, your faith, and the person God is shaping you to become. The horizon does not come into view because every distraction disappears. It comes into view because you finally decide where your attention belongs.

Bridge

From Return to Horizon

Return brings you back to what is true. Back to yourself. Back to peace. Back to faith. Back to the quiet places inside you that life, pressure, survival, and performance may have covered but could not destroy.

There is something sacred about that return. It does not mean everything is finished. It does not mean every wound has healed completely. It does not mean every question has been answered or every part of the future has become clear. It means you are no longer living as far away from yourself as you once were.

You have begun to recognize your own voice again. You have begun to breathe without apologizing. You have begun to understand that peace is not a luxury. It is part of how you live well.

You have begun to trust God not only when the answer arrives, but while the answer is still forming. That kind of return changes a person. It softens what pressure tried to harden. It steadies what fear tried to shake. It restores what survival tried to bury.

And once you begin returning to yourself, you are ready to live forward in a different way.

Not forward with panic.

Not forward with performance.

Not forward trying to prove that the difficult season did not affect you.

Forward with wisdom.

Forward with presence.

Forward with a clearer sense of what matters.

Forward with a spirit that has learned how to protect peace without closing the heart. This is where the horizon begins to feel different. It is no longer only a distant place you are trying to reach. It becomes a way of seeing. A way of living. A way of believing that your life still holds meaning beyond what has tilted, shifted, or changed.

A Juanderful Life is not simply about coming through difficulty. It is about becoming more awake because of what you have learned.

More honest.

More grounded.

More aligned.

More able to recognize beauty in ordinary days.

More willing to choose purpose over distraction.

More able to live from truth instead of performance.

The Horizon is the final movement of this journey. It is where awareness, navigation, and return begin to become a way of life.

Not a perfect life.

A conscious one.

A faithful one.

A life where you can look ahead without abandoning the present. A life where you can dream without denying what you have survived. A life where you can move forward with open eyes, open hands, and a steadier heart. You are not returning so you can stay still. You are returning so you can live forward whole.

PART IV: THE HORIZON

Chapter 13

LIVING AWAKE, NOT JUST ALIVE

Practicing Presence, Wonder, Gratitude, and Purpose

There is a difference between being alive and living awake. Being alive can happen by routine. You wake up. Move through the day. Answer what calls your name. Handle what needs handling.

Eat, work, speak, drive, plan, solve, sleep, and begin again. The body continues. The calendar fills. The responsibilities remain. But living awake asks something deeper. It asks whether you are present enough to notice the life you are moving through.

Not just manage it.

Not just survive it.

Not just improve it.

Notice it.

There are people who spend years living beside their own lives. They are close to beauty but too distracted to receive it. Close to love but too guarded to feel it. Close to purpose but too hurried to recognize it. Close to God but too noisy inside to hear the quiet invitations of grace.

A Juanderful Life is not only about reaching a destination. It is about becoming awake enough to experience the sacredness of the journey. That kind of awakening often begins in ordinary places.

The morning light across a table. The sound of someone you love laughing from another room. The smell of coffee. The quiet before the house begins moving. A familiar road. A small kindness.

A prayer whispered before the day becomes loud. These moments may not look important to the world, but they are often where life returns to us.

Wonder does not always arrive through grand experiences. Sometimes, wonder is simply the ability to see again. To look at something familiar and feel gratitude instead of numbness. To recognize that breath is still a gift. That peace is still possible.

That love is still worth receiving. That purpose can be found not only in large assignments, but also in the way we inhabit small moments with care.

Many people lose wonder because they are tired. Not because they are ungrateful. Not because they lack faith. But because pressure has trained their attention toward what is missing, urgent, broken, or unresolved. The mind becomes a scanner for problems. The spirit becomes accustomed to bracing.

The heart becomes careful. And slowly, life begins to feel less like something to be received and more like something to be managed. Living awake interrupts that pattern.

It says:

I will not let pressure make me blind to beauty.

I will not let disappointment make me unavailable to joy.

I will not let responsibility erase gratitude.

I will not let survival become the only language my life speaks.

Gratitude is not pretending everything is good.

It is noticing that goodness still exists.

Even in unfinished seasons.

Even in difficult chapters.

Even when life is not arranged exactly as you hoped.

Gratitude does not deny pain. It refuses to let pain become the only thing you can see. That is a powerful discipline. Because whatever receives your attention begins shaping your atmosphere.

If you only rehearse what is wrong, your spirit grows heavy. If you only measure what is missing, your life begins to feel empty even when blessings are present. If you only focus on what has not happened yet, you may miss what God is sustaining right now.

A Juanderful Life requires the courage to notice grace in real time. Not only afterward. Not only when the testimony is complete. Not only when the outcome makes sense. But now.

In the middle.

In the ordinary.

In the unfinished.

Presence is how gratitude becomes possible. You cannot be grateful for a life you are too distracted to inhabit. You cannot receive joy from a moment you keep rushing past.

You cannot recognize purpose if you are always measuring your life against someone else's pace. Living awake means returning your attention to what is true, sacred, and present.

It means asking:

What is here that I have stopped seeing?

What is good that I have been too tired to receive?

What is God showing me in this season that I might miss if I keep hurrying?

These questions slow the soul.

They do not remove responsibility.

They restore relationship with life.

Purpose also becomes clearer when you live awake.

Purpose is not always loud. Sometimes it is woven quietly into the way you love, serve, create, speak, forgive, build, and begin again.

Sometimes, purpose is found in the person you encourage. The room you make peaceful. The truth you finally tell. The gift you stop hiding. The wisdom you share because life taught it to you at a cost.

A Juanderful Life does not wait for purpose to appear only in dramatic assignments. It recognizes purpose in faithful presence. In showing up with a whole heart. In doing what is yours to do with love.

In allowing your life to become useful without becoming consumed. There is beauty in that. There is holiness in that. There is freedom in realizing that you do not have to chase significance if you are willing to live awake to what has already been placed in your hands.

Some people are alive but absent.

Absent from their joy.

Absent from their bodies.

Absent from their relationships.

Absent from their faith.

Absent from the quiet truth that life is happening now, not only someday when everything is finally complete. But the horizon is not only ahead of you. Sometimes it is within you. It is the widening of your vision. The softening of your spirit. The return of wonder.

The ability to say, even here, even now, there is still life to receive. That is what it means to live awake. Not perfectly. Not without sorrow. Not without responsibility. But with eyes open. Heart open. Spirit present. Faith alive.

A Juanderful Life is not merely a life that continues. It is a life that notices. A life that gives thanks. A life that makes room for wonder. A life that walks with purpose through ordinary days.

A life that refuses to become so busy surviving that it forgets to be grateful for the gift of being here. And sometimes, the most profound awakening begins with the simplest prayer: God, help me not to miss my life while I am trying to build it.

Chapter 14

SEEING BEYOND THE HORIZON

The Closing Vision of a Juanderful Life

There comes a point when the horizon no longer feels like something far away. It becomes something within you.

Not because every question has been answered.

Not because every wound has disappeared.

Not because life has become simple, predictable, or untouched by uncertainty. But because you have changed.

You have learned that a life can tilt without ending. You have learned that fear can speak loudly without becoming the final voice.

You have learned that drift can be noticed, weight can be named, peace can be protected, and faith can remain alive even while the future is still forming. That is the quiet miracle of a Juanderful Life.

It does not require perfection. It requires awakening. A Juanderful Life is a life lived with faith, presence, purpose, and peace. It is not a life free from disruption. It is a life that learns how to move through disruption without surrendering the soul.

It is a life where you stop measuring strength only by what you can carry. You begin measuring strength by what you can release.

What you can heal.

What you can forgive.

What you can protect.

What you can notice.

What you can become without losing tenderness.

Seeing beyond the horizon means understanding that your present moment is not the whole story. The difficulty you are facing is not the whole story. The disappointment you survived is not the whole story. The season that stretched you is not the whole story. The version of yourself that learned to survive is not the whole story. There is more.

More grace.

More wisdom.

More life.

More becoming.

More purpose still unfolding in places you may not yet recognize.

Sometimes the horizon is not a destination. Sometimes it is the ability to keep believing that life still holds meaning beyond what you can currently see.

That belief matters.

It keeps the heart from closing.

It keeps faith from becoming only memory.

It keeps peace from being postponed until every circumstance behaves.

It keeps purpose alive in ordinary days.

A Juanderful Life does not wait for life to become perfect before it becomes sacred. It recognizes sacredness here. In the unfinished. In the rebuilding.

In the quiet return.

In the breath after a hard season.

In the courage to begin again.

In the decision to live awake instead of merely alive.

There will still be storms.

There will still be questions.

There will still be moments when the path feels unclear. But now you know something deeper. You know how to pause.

How to listen.

How to return.

How to protect peace.

How to choose direction.

How to trust God while the picture is still forming.

You know that uncertainty does not have to erase identity.

You know that pressure does not have to steal presence.

You know that survival does not have to become your permanent home. This is the closing vision. Not a flawless life. A faithful one. Not a life without pain. A life that refuses to let pain become the only narrator.

Not a life arranged for applause. A life arranged around truth. Not a life where everything is always easy. A life where the soul can still breathe.

That is what makes it Juanderful. It is wonderful with wisdom in it. Wonderful with scars and grace. Wonderful with faith and honesty. Wonderful with discipline and softness.

Wonderful with tears that did not destroy you and joy that still found its way back. The horizon is not promising that nothing hard will come again. It is reminding you that you are no longer the same person who first felt the tilt.

You have learned to see differently.

You have learned to carry differently.

You have learned to live more awake.

And perhaps that is the gift.

Not that life never shifts.

But when it does, you can remain connected to what is true.

You can stand in the middle of uncertainty and still belong to yourself. You can walk with God through unfinished places and still trust that something sacred is forming. You can look ahead without needing to control every mile.

You can live with open hands.

Open eyes.

A steadier heart.

A softer spirit.

A clearer sense of what matters.

A Juanderful Life is not found beyond every problem. It is formed in the way you live through them. It is formed when you choose peace without denying pain.

When you choose faith without pretending certainty.

When you choose purpose without abandoning presence.

When you choose truth without losing tenderness.

When you choose to keep seeing beyond the horizon, even before the horizon fully appears. And so, you keep going.

Not frantic.

Not hollow.

Not asleep inside your own life.

Awake.

Present.

Faithful.

Aligned.

Still becoming.

Still believing.

Still seeing.

Because the horizon was never only about what was ahead of you. It was also about what was being restored within you. A Juanderful Life is a well-navigated life, rooted in faith, driven by purpose, and defined by repeated decisions that align with that purpose, not by the absence of storms.

A well-navigated life is not a life where every decision is easy. It is not a life where every door opens, every relationship stays whole, every plan unfolds neatly, or every prayer is answered in the way you expected.

It is a life where you learn how to move with wisdom when the path is not obvious. It is the ability to pause before panic. To listen before reacting. To tell the truth without letting the truth destroy your hope. To adjust without feeling like adjustment means failure.

Some people believe a wonderful life is measured by how little trouble enters it. But trouble visits every life in some form. The deeper question is not whether difficulty comes. The deeper question is whether difficulty takes over your direction.

A Juanderful Life means you remain connected to what matters even when life becomes demanding. You remember your values when pressure tries to make you forget them. You protect your peace without abandoning your responsibilities. You stay open to joy without pretending pain does not exist. You allow faith to steady you without using faith to deny reality.

This kind of life is not passive. It requires attention. It requires honesty. It requires the courage to notice when you are drifting, when you are bracing, when you are carrying too much, when you are moving too quickly to feel your own life.

It is not about control. It is about conscious direction. It is about becoming the kind of person who can be interrupted without being completely undone.

The kind of person who can be disappointed without becoming bitter. The kind of person who can be afraid without allowing fear to become the author of every decision. That is the heart of a Juanderful Life.

Not perfection. Not ease. Not constant happiness. A life lived awake. A life lived with faith, purpose, presence, and inner alignment. A life where even when the waters change, you do not completely lose yourself.

You have finally learned how to live a Juanderful Life!

About the Author

Jacqueline Boatwright-Daus, BS, MBA, Ed.S., IAT is an author, speaker, entrepreneur, childcare advocate, and faith-driven leader. Through her books, businesses, and ministry of encouragement, she helps individuals and families rise above life's challenges with clarity, courage, strategy, and purpose.

As the creator of the Juanderful brand, Jacqueline writes from a place of lived experience, faith, resilience, and vision. Her work encourages readers to steady their minds, strengthen their spirits, and keep moving forward when life tilts. Her Juanderful books are written to help readers lead, heal, rise, and live with faith, focus, and purpose.

www.ingramcontent.com/pod-product-compliance
Lightning Source LLC
Chambersburg PA
CBHW050001040726
47599CB00014B/1170

9780972529556